Rock Island Public Library
401 - 19th Street
Rock Island, IL 61201-8143

APR - - 2015

D1524240

WHAT FREEDOM SMELLS LIKE

A MEMOIR

AMY LEWIS

Anomaly Press
Los Angeles 2014

What Freedom Smells Like

Copyright © 2014 by Amy Lewis

All rights reserved. No part of this book may be reproduced or transmitted in any form or by any means without written permission of the author.

Published in the United States by Anomaly Press.

www.ReadAnomaly.com
www.WhatFreedomSmellsLike.com

ISBN 978-061-59344-19 (paperback)
ISBN 978-0-692-20647-8 (eBook)

Printed in the United States. Set in Garamond.

For Zora

Author's Note

I began writing this story many years ago when I realized memories of my relationship with Truth had begun the process of slipping away. I descended into meditative states going back to those years and jotted down all the details I remembered. I had hospital records, letters and session recordings to draw upon. After writing a few drafts, I placed all my notes in a box where the story lived in my garage for five years. The box kept speaking to me until I finally removed the top and accepted that I needed to publish the book.

Every scene in this memoir actually took place. I changed everyone's name to protect their anonymity except four – Truth's, George Anderson's, Eric's and my own.

Truth Lewis

"I know I am deathless. No doubt I have died myself ten thousand times before. I laugh at what you call dissolution, and I know the amplitude of time."

- Walt Whitman

Prologue

In two days, I will be a married woman. Again. I sink my toes into the sand and take a deep breath exhaling to the sound of the surf retreating. I adore the beach at night. Being a fair and freckled redhead, I only ever enjoy the sand after dark. The ocean possesses two elements that deeply turn me – wildness and power.

A rustic surfers' beach house, that we dubbed the love shack, sits behind me; we rented it for 4 days to host our family and friends for our Malibu beach wedding. My husband-to-be is playing taxi driver, picking up my parents from the airport. We are the quintessential LA couple – the struggling musician (him) marrying the struggling actress (me), only we don't struggle too much as we have a lucrative website to support us that I've run for eight years; it happens to be a porn site, and though that detail means little to me by this time, it meant much more years before.

I had ventured out to the surf at sunset with a tape measure to take precise measurements of how close we can seat our guests and not have them wash away with the tide. I have been thinking a lot about what washes away as my hometown, New Orleans, sits under water; it has been just 18 days ago since Katrina hit. My mom and dad lost their house; technically, their roof blew off but a house filled with water is as good as gone. Despite their muddy troubles, my mom insists, "You are not to cancel your wedding." They still planned to foot the bill for our celebration.

I lay back, molding a comfy pod in the sand and gaze upwards to the brilliant night sky. There are many ways to be washed away, to lose yourself in something greater. It can be a beautiful, ecstatic experience or a nightmare. Looking at my past, I seem to have preferred the latter. I must admit I am terrified I'll lose myself again in marriage. I suck in another deep breath and exhale slowly, enjoying my solitude.

Next month it will be six years since my husband Truth died. I have begun to forget exactly what he looked like. Not that I wouldn't recognize him if he came back from the dead and walked up to me, but the nuances, his scent, scars, voice, the details have faded with time. I rarely talk about him anymore, but a week ago I mentioned our relationship to a friend of mine.

"I'm so sorry you had to go through all that."

"I'm not. Losing him was the best thing that ever happened to me." I look up at her annoyed, as though she should know that.

It's a strange thing to say and I don't think he'd be mad at me for putting it that way. Besides, it's the truth. My relationship with my first husband could have started and ended with one night of passion; but for some reason, we both stuck in there rising from poverty to the members of the 1% club almost overnight before things began to spin out of control. Most curious of all – our relationship didn't even end when he died. Sometimes I don't think we get the real lessons, the priceless gemstones, until long after it's over, if we're willing to stick it out that long.

I've never been afraid of going to the raw edges of life; to be honest, it turns me on. But still, I am afraid of repeating the past. It seems like an utter waste of time. Making new mistakes, no problem, but the same old ones? I don't want my life to be made up of reruns.

At thirty-five, I finally understand that for me, the only relationship that truly matters is the one I have with myself. But knowing something and living it are two entirely different things. I have found so many ways to give myself away, to let myself get washed away with the emotional waves of my relationships. I never want to forget. I want to remember every moment, see it clearly, and know in my heart, that I'm not going back there again.

One

I never knew how Truth got his name. His mother named him Paul, but everyone called him Truth by the time that I met him, just as I was finishing my bachelor's degree at Berkeley. When I first laid eyes on him, I can't say I believed he was the man of my dreams, much less the man who would be the catalyst for my spiritual awakening. I simply thought, *I wouldn't mind sleeping with him*. What a sight: tall, black, bald, sexy as all hell, covered from head to toe in black tribal art and piercings; he looked like he should be put on a pedestal and displayed in a gallery.

Truth was a regular at Larry Blakes, a restaurant and Berkeley institution since the 1940's, with a bar and music club downstairs. I worked there as a waitress. He noticed me as well, and we began a game of mutual flirtation with smiles and over the head glances. Weeks after our first meeting, he approached me on my break and asked if I wanted to go out. Just before I could utter yes, I remembered my boyfriend. A lawyer in San Francisco named Joshua, we had been dating for almost a year. I was a good girl, and good girls don't have two boyfriends at once. It's in our official handbook, on page 72. I politely declined.

Still, I secretly watched him. He glided down Telegraph Avenue, always in hurry, always with a purpose. He floated in and out, a hug here, a quick smile there, a kiss on the cheek and then off to this meeting or that appointment. Always places to go, people to see, and too little time for Truth. Everyone knew him. He couldn't walk two blocks down Telegraph without at least five people coming up to him for a hug or that special *brotha* handshake white men never could quite get right. I loved how everyone noticed him.

My mind likes to put people into compartments when I first meet them. I don't think I'm alone in this. But Truth had this quality that made it hard to place him in a box. If I had to classify him, I'd say one part gangster, one part grifter, and one part artist, packaged together with intelligence and charm.

In May of 1995, a week before my graduation, my boyfriend, the lawyer I almost forgot, who defended San Quentin inmates at their parole hearings, dumped me on a bench in Golden Gate Park. He said something about me not being thin enough. After that, I stopped listening. Curiously, I never cared about what other people thought about my appearance, a trait I inherited from Dad. I knew I appeared beautiful at times, because men and women had told me. But my weight was another issue – a very sensitive one. I wasn't obese, but a far cry from the "skinny" that many men desire, and that I too I coveted. I was a sensualist in a world where deprivation seemed a necessity to look good on the outside. I enjoyed the taste of food almost as much as the taste of a man. And, I had a hard time saying no to myself. What did he say again? He had some polite euphemism, something suggesting I didn't take very good care of myself. He was right. I didn't know the first thing about taking care of myself, but it didn't matter in those days. Maybe it should have. I was a natural redhead with fire engine red hair, and I had been informed by every man I had ever been with (I could count them on one hand, barely) that I was a great lover, extra pounds and all. I sat on the park bench alone after he left, smugly believing he would miss my company. In the chain of events leading up to Truth, two events had to occur. This dumping of my sexy, pudgy ass on a park bench in Golden Gate Park was the first.

I had graduated from Berkeley the day before; my parents came from New Orleans for the event and were returning home. I waited with them as they checked in their bags at the packed airport counter.

"I can't wait to have you back at home."

I smiled stiffly as my mom hugged me. We had a loving yet formal relationship with a whole lot kept hostage under the surface. I always thought it was a result of her being British and learning that wonderfully English way of relating. Anything you don't like or can't deal with – just smile and ignore it.

After saying our goodbyes, I sat on the back hood of my beat up Nissan in the airport parking lot watching the sunset and the planes ascend. With my degree from prestigious university, my parent's job of seeing me through college was now done. I planned to return home to New Orleans in five weeks, work for a year while studying for the GREs, and apply for PhD programs in clinical psychology. I wanted to be a psychologist and work in academia. I had my future all figured out. Now I had five weeks to enjoy myself in Berkeley.

As I watched the sun go down, I remembered a moment at thirteen, sitting on my windowsill overlooking the street in Gretna, a suburban neighborhood outside of New Orleans. There were five different model homes in my neighborhood. You had your pick of five different floor plans and accompanying childhoods. I gazed longingly out – my world began where the comfort of my middle class home ended. I wondered when my life would actually start because I knew it had not yet. Now ten years later, I had a clear sense that the moment had arrived. And I had an even clearer sense it arrived because I was choosing it – willing it. Life started now. The real clock, I could hear the ticking.

Energized and excited, I felt my car pulled along the freeway, catapulting me into something I could not explain and could not resist. I was twenty-three, done with school, and ready to begin my life. I had a 9 p.m. shift at Blakes. I had started working as host and cocktail waitress about eight months before but quickly moved up the ranks to waitress and part time accountant; I really wanted the coveted job of bartender. I was generally introverted and quiet, but I felt comfortable there.

On that Tuesday night, I covered for a friend's cocktail shift. While it was stressful being in the horde of drunks, it was an important job – inebriating the coeds so they could bare their souls and bodies to the man or woman next to them. As the Counting Crows bellowed out of the speakers, I maneuvered my way through a packed room like a prima ballerina, my tray filled with glasses held daintily above my head. Usually a bit of a klutz, with much practice, I had mastered tray balancing. Surrounded by drunk and unsteady people, I felt in control and strong.

I saw Truth sitting at the counter, talking to the bartender, Mel, a gorgeous six-foot tall brunette grad student who had been to Cuba. I'm not exactly sure why she had gone to Cuba; I assumed a political or humanitarian mission. Normally such a beautiful and intelligent creature would intimidate me, but not Mel. She took a liking to me, maybe sensing I wanted to emulate her. I put down my tray, and while Mel mixed the next round of drinks, I sat on the one empty bar stool – right next to Truth.

Neither Truth nor I enjoyed chit chatting. Our attraction was immediate and intense. I might have been a good girl, but I was not coy, and my good girl handbook said nothing about celibacy.

"I'm officially single."

He smiled a warm, sexy smile. "What time do you get off?"

"Supposed to be 2 a.m. but since I'm working a double to-morrow maybe I can change it to midnight."

"I'll meet you back here at midnight. Right here at this stool." He stood up and traced his hand over the stool tracing the outline of where his butt had been. He said goodbye to Mel; she blew him a kiss as he walked out into the night.

I sat for a minute before picking up the tray to deliver drinks. I had a date with Truth! Truth wants to meet *me* for a drink. My stomach swirled with desire. I talked JT, the night manager, into letting me off early, went down to the locker room to freshen up, and surveyed myself in the mirror. Wearing my favorite pair of black sailor pants, a sleeveless white blouse and black velvet vest on top, I knew I would never be a Mel, but I looked pretty good. I felt good too. Feeling satisfied, I held my breath, closed my eyes and jumped.

I landed next to the designated bar stool and found a napkin taped to the red vinyl seat, *Reserved For The Sexy Redheaded Waitress* written in blue ink and a drink on the bar – my favorite, Amaretto Sour. Holly, a blonde waitress a few years younger than me, sat at the next bar stool, ordering an after-work beer.

"So you and Truth, huh …" she glanced over at me and smiled. Word traveled fast at Blakes.

Truth had worked as a bouncer for Blakes in the past, and they considered him part of the family. I grinned as I sipped my drink, enjoying the sweetness rolling over my tongue. I hadn't bonded with too many women at the restaurant. I've always felt more comfortable with men. Holly, with her long hair and indie girl energy seemed at ease. She spent a long time looking me over.

"He's something else, that one," she said as she went back to her Guinness.

"Is he? I'm just getting to know him." I wondered what she meant.

"Brian doesn't like him but he's got his reasons…" She laughed "One time his date ended up leaving with Truth. Not hard to believe."

Brian, one of the owners of the restaurant, always seemed to have a different girlfriend.

"I like him myself … only I don't really like what he does."

"And what is that?" She had my full attention.

"He used to share a house with one of my friends. I can't say exactly what he's into but she said he had a mighty large collection of firearms. Once when I dropped her off, his door was slightly ajar and I peeped inside; I saw him cleaning them all laid out on his bed …"

Before she could finish telling me what happened, Truth breezed in through the front door. He had to jockey around a big group of French students. He moved swiftly through them, breaking up conversations as he forced his way through the packed crowd, never once breaking eye contact with me.

"Have fun, sweetie." Holly winked at me with a little too much worldliness for her age, taking the remains of her drink with her as she walked downstairs.

"So you came back." He stood next to my barstool, towering over me with his sexy grin, wearing a maroon sleeveless t-shirt, and army green Dickies.

"Did you have any doubts I wouldn't?"

"No." He smiled "I was just hoping you didn't find a new boyfriend since we last spoke … since you only have one at a time."

"Nope, I'm still single." I took an ice cube in my mouth and sucked it, awash in my feminine power. I peered into his dark brown eyes as he stood a few inches from me. My body felt light headed and giddy. *Doesn't like what he does. What the hell did that mean?* I was not the first young woman to be turned on by mystery and danger. I couldn't resist him, and even if I could, I didn't want to.

We walked down to the Rat, what they called the downstairs basement. The space looked grimy and the music blared and as we descended into a cloud of cigarette smoke: an up and coming Ska band held the attention of most of the audience. Truth handed me a pool stick as he trotted off to the bar to get us another round.

I'll admit I didn't know what I was doing – in playing pool and playing with Truth. I found it fun to surrender to someone and something bigger than I was.

I downed the last sip of my second drink and, wiping the amaretto from my lips, I leaned over to Truth and cooed, "You're coming home with me tonight, but I bet you're already aware of that."

Boldness was not difficult for me; I just didn't feel inspired to do it very often.

We tried not to wake any of the six Berkeley women I lived with, tiptoeing up the stairs to my bedroom. I enjoyed the choice room in the back of the house, with hardwood floors and a view of all the branches of a giant oak tree in the backyard. I threw a scarf over my lamp, giving the room a warm, golden glow and switched on the CD player, which held Bjork's debut album, my second copy since I had played my first copy into the ground. Her childlike voice broke the silence in the room.

I invited Truth to sit down on my clean, crisp white down comforter. I had only lived in this room for six months, and he was the first man to sit on my bed.

I turned back to Bjork and let her sensual voice fill me as I began a slow, tantalizing dance as Truth watched. I felt myself take charge of the room, confident of my womanly charms, but I couldn't take my siren song too seriously, and after a few minutes broke into giggles. He smiled, watching me try to seduce him, knowing full well who was seducing whom. He understood I liked to be in control and he let me.

I took his hand and stood him up, removing his brown, corduroy coat. I put my face into the fabric, inhaling deeply, smelling his scent up close for the first time. His skin smelled foreign and intoxicating. It wasn't cologne, but Truth's body; a strong, piercing scent like a deep woodsy musk, body oil, mixed with some sweat with a slight sweetness. I had been with five men before Truth, and all of them doused so much cologne, their true scent remained a mystery. I took off his sleeveless t-shirt and flung it to the ground dramatically, running my hands over his chest. His muscles were defined, and I liked the way my whiteness contrasted when pressed against his black skin. A thick five-inch scar extended over his right side; I asked about it as I ran my fingers over the long bump. He smiled, taking my hand up to his mouth, kissing my finger. I turned him round, running my fingers over his back, over the tattoo of a huge black panther that appeared like it was about to attack a sailor girl whose large breasts looked like they had been covered up as an afterthought. With his belt buckle in my hand, he stopped me.

"I want to see you first."

Without breaking eye contact, I let him take off my clothes. His eyes reflected none of the disappointment that I felt when I looked at my 150-pound body in the mirror. I stilled my mind and allowed my body to revel in his touch. I let him turn me round and run his hands up and down and over my skin. His hands felt smooth. Smiling, he imitated me sticking his nose in my skin and taking big whiffs. He explored each limb, one at a time, running his hands, lips and tongue over my skin, returning his eyes back to me after each exploration.

I had long since blissfully given over control to him.

He laid me out on my empty bed and continued his sensual explorations. I closed my eyes and took a deep breath and inhaled his scent again. Now, his smell made me uncomfortable – like a traveler to a new country who didn't speak the language yet, nervous because it didn't smell like anything she'd known. I took a deep breath, and I let myself relax into the unknown; I let myself lose control, to enjoy exploring and being explored. As Bjork crooned "Venus as a Boy" into the air, he unzipped his pants. They landed on the floor next to mine.

Truth lay sleeping when I woke up the next morning. I peered down and noticed his toes poking out from under the white sheet. I didn't like his toes. I've always had a thing about toes. Very few do I really like, they have to be well manicured. I'm not so picky about other body parts; toes are the exception. I don't even like my own except occasionally when I catch them in a certain light. His toes had not been manicured in a long time, and the big toenail was a little bit longer than the top of the toe. *What the hell am I doing?* I wondered if I had just made a huge mistake. The rest of his body was beautiful: sculpted, smooth and covered in art. His toes seemed like they didn't belong to his body, and it dawned on me that I was in bed with a stranger.

He opened his eyes and smiled at me like he had been awake the whole time, watching me look at his feet. "Good morning mon petit tete rouge."

My heart skipped a beat. I laughed. Only his toes bothered me; the rest of him suited me just fine.

Two

Romance ensued. We established a routine for the first three weeks. We would wake up and eat breakfast together, and then I dropped him off at campus so he could work, the exact nature of his work remained a mystery. I'd go to my part time day job as a personal assistant. I'd do errands, workout, and five nights of the week I had the dinner or late shift at Blakes. He usually showed up at the restaurant about 7p.m. hanging out in the Rat or around Telegraph until I got off, at which time we'd go back to my place.

One night in our third week of dating, I left work at midnight and a large, black homeless woman approached wearing a long purple skirt and an oversized navy hooded sweat-shirt. I recognized her. She usually sat around the corner on Durant.

"Hey, you, Amy? You must be her. I ain't seen such red hair on anybody else."

"Uhh yeah. Hi." How did she know my name?

"Come on, girl, let's go. I got no time to dawdle." She started walking quickly ahead of me. I smiled when I realized Truth had sent her to walk me to my car.

"You got a good man. I had one too, back in the day. But that was long ago. A longggg time ago."

She belted out a laugh, loud and croaky. She walked while rooting through a hot pink tote bag. "Hey, girl, this is your color." She pulled out a teal scarf and held it up to my hair, grinning, which exposed brown teeth that looked like they hadn't been brushed in ten years. The scarf and other items she removed from her bag were for sale. I gave her two dollars for a pair of shorts and thanked her.

"So did he say when I'd be seeing him?"

"Girrllll, you think I'm his secretary?" She let out a loud raucous laugh as she turned back up Telegraph.

I started my car and gazed at myself in the rearview mirror. I smiled, feeling warm all over; I felt looked after, important and special, and loved completely by this mysterious man, who was so different from everyone else in my life.

As I drove through the empty streets of Berkeley, I pushed Holly's story to the back of my head. I couldn't believe we had only been dating for a few weeks. My mind flashed to the day after our first night together. He came to see me at the restaurant as I hosted the lunch shift, carrying a single white rose, and asked if he could see me again. I said I needed to think about it.

"Think about what?" he asked.

"If I want to fall in love with you."

"You do that and get back to me with your conclusion, professor."

"Hey wait … I am kidding." He was already out the door.

The next day I found him walking down Telegraph. I came up from behind him putting my arms around his waist. He turned quickly, somewhat startled.

"Look, I'm an idiot sometimes. I say stupid things when I'm scared."

"Yeah?"

"Yeah."

15

"When are you gonna stop being afraid?"

"I'm not sure. What time is it now?"

He smiled. "Come here." He pulled me over to a mural painted on the wall of Amoeba records and leaning up against it he took me into his arms, gingerly cupping his huge hands on my cheeks. "You don't have to be afraid of anything. I can't believe this myself. I did not plan for us to happen." And looking down at me, he kissed me – the most luxurious, soft, soothing kiss ever.

I took a deep breath into his chest and began to let go. It felt like the right thing to do. Standing on the Avenue in his arms, it seemed like the only thing to do.

I arrived back at my house, and I saw Truth waiting out front, smoking a red Basic.

"Hey, you, where have you been?" I called out the window as I parked.

"I thought I'd be working late, but we finished early so I got a ride."

I walked over to him on the front steps, and I sat down leaning my head on his shoulders, letting out a sigh.

"You should have knocked on the door. My roommates would have let you in."

"I didn't want to wake any one up. You look tired, sweetness. Let's get you into bed." He stroked my hair that was sweaty from the June heat. My neck arched back slightly with each stroke. I relaxed instantly.

"What do you do when we're not together?"

He continued running his fingers all the way down to the bottom of my shoulder length locks. "A little bit of this and a little bit of that."

I wanted to find out how he made his money. I knew he pierced people. I had seen him do piercing more than once and a number of the staff at Blakes had their belly button rings put in by Truth. He had pierced people right up on the pool table. He had lived in France for the last two years with a French woman, Lea, and had only been back in Berkeley for a few months. I knew so little about his past.

"If you don't have a job right now, you can tell me."

"Sweetheart… let's go to bed … we'll talk later. I promise." He scooped me up, grabbed my bag and walked up to my house and into the bedroom. The next morning, I gave Truth a key so in the future he didn't have to wait outside.

Three days later, I got home about 9 p.m. from the dinner shift and found Truth sitting alone, in the corner of my room in darkness. He stared silently out the window and didn't even notice me as I walked in.

"What's wrong?" I kept the lights off and went to him. He didn't say anything. His eyes came back from wherever they had been, and he looked at me, putting his hand on my face.

"Are you ok?"

"My mom died today."

"What?" We had never talked about his family. She had been battling brain cancer for the last year. She was the reason he had come back from France.

"I am so sorry. God, I am sorry." I didn't know what else to say. I held out my arms in the dark and I pulled his body close to mine. He didn't cry. He was still and quiet. We sat together in silence.

"I can't go to her funeral. If I go, then I'll kill someone there."

"I understand." Of course, I didn't. I could not conceive of not going to my mother's funeral. Who was he going to kill?

I took him to bed, undressed him, tenderly stroking his soft skin with my fingertips while blowing little butterfly kisses up and down his chest. I did my best to keep his mind off of his grief. It made me incredibly sad to see him like this. I sensed he did not want to talk about his family, so I kept my questions to myself.

From that day on, we spent every night together. He knew my plans were to go back to New Orleans on the 23rd of June, but we didn't discuss it. A week before my departure date, we woke up late on Sunday and went to Sproul Plaza on campus to a drum circle. A hodge-podge of students, hippies, Africans and Rastafarians played djembe and other drums while girls with no shoes or bras and long flowing hair danced in the center. I loved Berkeley, and would miss the city dearly. I adored the hippie leftovers fresh out of the Museum of Bekerlydom. During my tenure in the early nineties, students were the least politically active ever. Most young people didn't care anymore. We had our right to free speech but chose to talk about getting drunk, fucking or how we would never make as much money as our parents.

The Internet would not boom for a few years; the economy looked stale. I marched once in a demonstration – for Rodney King. Well, technically I marched. In reality, the buses weren't running, and I had to get home, so I walked along with the demonstrators to my apartment. "No Justice, No Peace," I shouted. I liked shouting.

We sat on the steps of Sproul Plaza, birthplace of free speech, listened to the drums, and Truth began talking about growing up in Berkeley. One of his uncles had run a successful real estate business, and in the sixties he let the Black Panthers use the office upstairs for meetings. His parents knew Angela Davis; she even babysat for him once. Some of his family had been involved in the movement. His father was an alcoholic and their marriage ended when Truth turned eight. His first step-dad, also an alcoholic, abused his mom, his sister and him. Truth left home as a teenager, after threatening to kill his stepfather if he ever touched his mother again. He cared for himself from a young age, even living on the streets for a while. He met an older, wealthy woman who took a liking to him, and he lived with her.

"She was your sugar Mama? You slept with her, right?"

"Beat living on the street. I was sixteen. You have no idea the shit I saw."

I put my head down on his shoulder listening to the drums and trying to imagine his life.

"I joined the Army, but before I left I met a girl – we were eighteen. She got pregnant, so I married her. I have two kids by her, both girls."

He had mentioned his children a few times before. "When was the last time you saw them?"

"Been a while." He gazed out at the drum circle, his brown eyes far away. "The army sent me over to Grenada and later El Salvador. I saw combat and came back confused and not adjusted.

One minute I'm in the middle of a jungle with an automatic machine gun and the next I'm in a burger joint in Antioch, California - a fucking 'burb littered with white picket fences. They just dropped us back off in the states as Civilians. I got into some trouble. This guy at the fucking burger place said something to Kathy – about us being together."

"She was white."

"Yeah, a blonde from a small town in the Central Valley. I lost it. Went nuts on this fucker, and I did some time at Pelican Bay. When they released me, I run into this guy at a bar. He said he could use someone with my background. So I started to work for him. One job led to another; eventually I ended up doing some assignments for the NSA."

"The what?"

"The National Security…"

"I know what the letters stand for. You worked for them? Doing what? I don't understand."

"Special Assignments."

I lifted my head off his shoulder and noticed for the first time how bright the sun was. I squinted my eyes while trying to digest his words. "Special Assignments? Like … ?"

"Different things … I watch people; collect data, study their habits, movements … and sometimes I take care of problems."

I remembered Holly's story about going to his place, seeing the guns. *I don't like what he does, but I like him.* Is this what she meant?

"You don't want to hear about this, and I don't want to scare you. I've led an unusual life."

I did not believe him. Was he even allowed to tell me he was in the NSA? Does the NSA exist? Yes. Well, I think so. I guess so. Assuming it exists, people work for them, right? Ok, I said to myself, sure.

I remembered a man I met four years before at Depaul Hospital in New Orleans. I had a breakdown at eighteen and was hospitalized for five weeks. He was good looking in a Richard Dreyfus sort of way, in his mid-fifties, average height with receding salt and pepper hair. He seemed kind, intelligent, dignified; he shuffled when he walked, perhaps from the medication. My friends on the psych ward told me he was an assassin. He had worked for the government for a long time, and one day he snapped. He couldn't do it any longer, and since that was all he'd ever done, he didn't know how to live. To resolve the conflict he decided to kill himself, and we ended up on the same floor. He received heavy Electroconvulsive therapy and had permission to skip the groups, which was too bad, because everyone wanted to hear his stories.

One night at the hospital, I retreated to the sunroom; my day had been difficult, and I had been crying while talking to a fellow patient about never being able to love anyone and he must have overheard. He shuffled in, saw me and smiled, and I guess, not wanting to disturb me, said a quick hello and shuffled out. He walked slow, heavy footed, and I could hear his footsteps drag across the carpet. The sound of his steps stopped. I heard them coming back. He stood in the doorway.

"If I were a younger man, my dear, I'd fall for you." We smiled. We had a moment - a real moment. Then he shuffled back out.

He was an agent, an assassin, and we had a thing – a brief thing, but an encounter all the same. Maybe I'm attracted to assassins. Maybe they're attracted to me. I rationalized to myself couldn't Truth have worked for the NSA and perhaps even "taken care of problems" as he put it? It was possible I guessed.

Still I had doubts. I had met a friend of my sister's at a Saints game the last time I'd visited New Orleans before meeting Truth. He worked for the FBI. I wonder if I should call him and ask him about the NSA? Could he look up Truth's name?

I didn't call. I felt too stupid. As the days passed, my doubts faded. He received strange phone calls at my place in Berkeley. And I found pages of code in his notebook – page after page. I sneaked a look at the notebook in his backpack. What did all this mean?

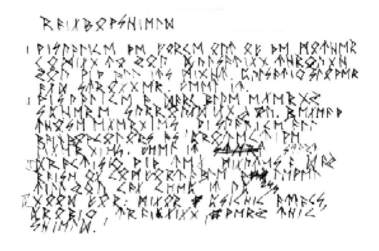

I told Frida, one of my roommates, about what he did. She had spent a good amount of time with Truth since he stayed with me every night and didn't doubt the story for a second. She was very level headed. "That's pretty exciting," I agreed. It was all pretty fucking crazy. And "crazy" excited me.

"When we talked yesterday …" I asked him a day later as we drove around in the rain running errands. "You said you took care of problems. What does that mean?"

"They hand you an assignment. A folder with photos, a name and you find the person. You observe them. You spend a lot of time patiently watching. You discover their routine, their mannerisms, pace, energy, how long it takes them to pee in the bathroom, their regular acquaintances, their usual route; eventually you get to know them better than they know themselves." I stared out the window as we drove down College Avenue past the upscale trendy boutiques and restaurants. I gazed at the big drops of water forming on the glass, merging and falling into each other. I wondered if he was here to watch someone? Did he study someone when we weren't together? Getting to know them better than they knew themselves?

"You do it quickly, making it appear like an accident."

I didn't want to hear that. An accident. I took a deep breath. Is he for real?

"You mean, you kill them?"

"Amy, every day people die all over the globe, important people, bad people; mostly men who are responsible for a lot of pain in this world. Many times you never hear about it. When you read about someone - a person high up in business or politics - dying, do you think it's always of natural causes, just an accident or a suicide? Sometimes yes, other times, it only looks that way."

The fact that the man I loved might be an assassin was not what bothered me. Hell, it turned me on. What bothered me was that it all sounded so incredulous. This kind of shit that only happens in the movies. I could not figure out if he was for real. I recalled what Holly said, I remembered the code in his book, and I thought well, maybe so.

My life had been so predictable up until meeting Truth. A simple check list of events: attend high school, get good grades, get accepted to a good college, have a breakdown (the one exception to the predictability), take proper meds, get lots of therapy, recover, go to college, get good grades, find a job, a man, and one day a house and babies. I sensed life should not be predictable. My instincts told me this world held many secrets beyond my wildest dreams, but I had been afraid to open myself up. Always scared. If I had had a German grandmother (which I didn't), she would most certainly have called me an angsthase – a fear bunny.

This exciting, smart, and sexy as all hell, larger than life man wanted me. He wanted me, and I wanted him, so why not? Why the hell not? I liked his foreignness, his mystery because predictability bored me to tears. I didn't care what he did or had done. With him, I felt safe from the world. So I rolled down the window to my red Nissan as we drove in the rain past the post office, and I threw my doubts away for anyone, who might need them, to catch. I watched as they fell into the water collecting on the edge of the curb and floated towards the sewer drain. I didn't need my apprehension. I believed Truth.

"Do you want to keep working for them?"

"I'm not sure, I think it would be good to take a break for a while. Do something different. I didn't plan on returning to this country. Quite honestly, I'd like to move back to France. I hate this place."

"What do you think about coming back to New Orleans with me? It's sort of like France ... well ok, not really but there is the French food . . . I'm being selfish. I know it's crazy. We've only been together a grand total of four weeks. I don't want to be without you. Not forever – just a bit of time while we both figure things out. You said yourself you could use a break. What do you think?"

"And what would I do in New Orleans?"

"We could both get jobs, find a place together. We'll figure it out."

In my world, saying "we'll figure it out" was an entirely plausible plan. I usually fell on my feet and got what I wanted. In my selfish desire for Truth, I didn't spend one minute thinking about what New Orleans would be like for him. I closed my eyes and saw only what I wanted to see.

A week later, as planned, I drove to Los Angeles where my sister, Julie, flew to meet me; we traveled cross-country with all my stuff crammed into the trunk and back seat. Ten days later, after Truth completed his business in Berkeley, he planned to take a Greyhound Bus to meet me.

Little did I know how close he came to never arriving. Much later, I would find his notebook with nine unsent letters written to me from those days we were apart. He would start a letter sometimes getting four paragraphs in, another letter just one paragraph, another one just two sentences …

He addressed them all the same "Hello My Dearest Amy." He always capitalized the first character in every word of his writing.

"It's Been Only Days Since I've Held Your Body Tightly Against Mine, Yet I Miss You More Than The Day Before. Tell Me Have You Found Another To Fill Your Bed, Your Heart And Your Head?"

In another letter he broke up with me: "Perhaps It Would Be Best If We Both Returned To Our Respective Homes And, If After We've Both Finished Our Pressing Business, We Can Meet Again In Another Country At Another Time."

And another message was different: "Yes My Love I'm In Love With You. You Are In That Place Within Me Where Only A Few Have Been Before … And Moving So Swiftly To A Place Where I have Been Alone For Such A Long Time. And, I Welcome This Feeling With Open Arms."

The next written three days later: "Amy I don't Think Either Of Us Are Ready To Be In A Monogamous Relationship … Besides I Really Don't Think." That one ended there.

He never showed me the letters, but he got on the Greyhound Bus and four days later, arrived in New Orleans. Getting on the bus was the second thing that had to occur for this story to come into being. And it happened.

Three

Y ou know how sometimes you have a thought to say something, so your brain sends the instructions to your vocal chords but before the message gets there, the situation changes. You can't stop the signal so you say it anyway. And now, the words seem out of place and weird. That's how we ended up in New Orleans. I planned out my future when I only had to think about myself. After meeting Truth I hadn't bothered to cancel the plan and reconsider. Or you could just call me selfish.

I needed a year off to work and gain life experience before going to graduate school. That's how I spun my plan at least; in reality, my last semester at college I began to have serious doubts about being a starving student for another five years. I began to question whether I even wanted to be a psychologist.

I studied and excelled in psychology because I understood the terrain. My "breakdown," at eighteen taught me a few things.

I had a bumpy transition from girlhood to womanhood. When I turned sixteen, I had a sexual affair with my sister's 29 year old boyfriend. I consented so far as you can consent when you're curious and young and never held a boy's hand before. The affair started in the sticky heat of a New Orleans summer, on a long thin strip of green grass that separated two identical suburban houses. The cicadas and mosquitoes filled the air with their chirping and thrumming. I returned to my house across the street and turned on the lights in my bedroom; I saw that I was covered in pink mosquito bites – covered in *every* conceivable place on my body.

Almost immediately, I started to have a lot of very bad feelings about myself. I was a whore, an evil slut, a woman not to be trusted, a woman who steals things and people; who steals her sister's boyfriend. Like all women who do such things, I needed to be punished. That's what I thought. The mosquito bites were a sign of my badness. I began to scratch, and the pain felt good. Days later, as the welts healed, my body still itched, like an emotion inside me needed to get out but didn't know how. I started clawing at my skin, hoping it would be released. I scratched my scalp at first, hoping the feeling might reside there. Then down my legs, stomach and arms. When the scratching ceased to alleviate my guilt, I started cutting myself.

The affair with my sister's boyfriend consisted of three experiences. The fact that I went back for the second and third time seemed proof of my guilt. I couldn't handle the fact that I loved the pleasure and willingly returned for more. My therapist and every self-help book I read wanted to paint me as a victim due to my age. Calling me a victim or survivor of abuse took away all my power. Confused? Yes. Naïve? Yes. In over my head? Perhaps. But Victim? No. As a teenager with a heightened desire for sensual experiences, I could be placed in only two boxes: a slut that should feel ashamed or a victim who deserved pity and protection. Never wanting to limit my options, I teetered between both depending on the company.

The first time cutting was an accident. My cat scratched me, and later that day, I noticed the red coagulated blood on my face in a mirror at Maison Blanche, a department store. I liked the way it looked. I started doing it myself, first with knives and later with the razor blades I bought in a box; they offered greater precision. I liked watching the blood leak from my body. Perhaps the bad feelings were in the blood cells and would leak out. I liked attending to the cut, wiping it with antiseptic, covering the wound with a protective bandage. I was as gentle in the attending to my wounds as I had just been harsh in causing them.

After about six months of cutting, now 17 and a senior in high school, it took me three days to get up the nerve to talk to my parents. I sat down on their bed as they watched a rerun of *Mash* and stared at their headboard.

"I want to go talk to someone. Like a therapist."

I didn't tell them why. They could see something was wrong even though I kept my cuts hidden and my mouth shut. I can only imagine what I put my parents through. My parents realized I had "problems" and they knew about the affair with my sister's boyfriend, but they were overwhelmed and ill equipped to help me. I was wound up—a ball of repressed rage, desire and pain, best handled by professionals.

The cutting grew into an addiction. I wore long sleeves and kept this secret from everyone, except my therapist. I had no idea at the time this ritual was practiced by young (mostly white) girls all over America. I knew enough to realize my behavior was not normal. My cutting habit, coupled with a four-month stretch of depression, where I barely slept or ate and had nightmares regularly, landed me in the hospital. In no uncertain terms my therapist said if I didn't check myself in, he would commit me. I was in no state to argue. In the summer after graduating from

High School, instead of packing for college and saying goodbye to friends, I checked into a mental hospital.

Locked up, for the first time I experienced a little freedom in my mind. In the hospital I could release and be myself. The label of mental patient gave me a great deal of room to breathe. Up until then, I had always been holding my breath. I shamelessly acted out with the staff; compared to the introverted girl who repressed everything, this seemed like progress. When my regular therapist went on vacation, I bragged to my fellow inmates: *I'm gonna chew up and spit out the therapist they send in to see me.* I was arrogant, destructive and completely unaware that hurting other people would only hurt me. Or maybe I was completely aware and just didn't give a fuck. In the treatment team progress notes, my psychiatrist wrote:

She is describing to me something that sounds like a dissociative phenomenon. She dissociates cognitive events – i.e. specific memories, but retains with intensity the affect. This results in feelings with no explanation for their origin and her feeling depersonalized and disorganized. She can look at this in terms of a transient psychotic state.

They diagnosed me with Major depression (somewhat resolved) and severe Borderline Personality Disorder (BPD). At age eighteen, half the women I knew in the South seemed borderline, so my diagnosis hardly seemed distinctive.

BPD is described as a personality disorder characterized by extreme instability and impulsivity, fear of abandonment and self-injurious behavior as well as by extreme 'black and white' thinking, mood swings, emotional reasoning, disrupted relationships and difficulty in functioning in a way society accepts as normal.

While I acknowledged not liking the anguish I felt, I didn't want to give any of it up to the doctors. I was not about to surrender and give up my "personality" defect. I spat on the diagnosis. Tuah. Tuah. I spat on the hospital. I said *I am a passionate woman. I feel deeply. I love deeply. I live my life full out, and I apologize for nothing.* I considered a mental diagnosis a badge of honor. It meant I was really living.

The psychiatric disorders I studied at Berkeley were more than case histories. I had lots of crazy friends. If I hadn't suffered from a disorder myself, I knew someone who did.

(X) Borderline personality disorder (me)
(X) Major Depression (me again)
(X) Bipolar (Marge & Bertie)
(X) Schizophrenia (Corey)
(X) Narcissistic Personality Disorder (Trent)
(X) Anorexia and Bulimia (too many to name)
(X) Brief Reactive Psychosis (Mr. Samuels)

Studying the causes and treatments for these disorders fascinated me. When we learned one of the side effects of ECT included memory loss, it wasn't just a fact to be regurgitated on a test. I recalled the jokes we played when I was in the hospital, on the ECT patients, right after they finished a treatment.

"Hey, Miss Carol, where's my pack of cigarettes? You said you'd buy me a pack of cigarettes because you smoked ALL of mine last night … don't you remember?"

"Oh … I did … I'm so sorry, dawlin' … I don't know where my head is tonight."

We'd fall over laughing. "We don't know where your head is either – maybe you should ask the doctors what they did to it!" Miss Carol would start laughing too, still not sure what had really happened. Most ECT patients could remember little of the events in the hours before.

My senior year thesis project explored the use of "labeling" psychiatric disorders as a form of social control and about the stigma attached to being called 'mentally ill'. I was painfully aware of how people reacted to me when I got out of the hospital – of my high school friends, who had no idea how to talk to me. I had no idea how to talk to them either. I understood what it felt like to be thought of as "crazy" when you knew you weren't, to have the doors locked behind you, your bags searched and baths monitored. It's a terrible feeling - not to be trusted.

Most of the people at DePaul were not "crazy", just in desperate need of new coping skills. Most of us had lost the ability to pretend everything was ok. It was the first time I remember feeling free to be myself – no matter what that looked like. And strangely enough, I also had a lot of fun. One afternoon a bunch of us sat in the break room, bored and looking for some trouble. It was the first room the visitors saw when entering the locked down facility. A long set of tables filled the room, and craft supplies sat in various baskets. DePaul was an expensive, private hospital, nice by any standard and certainly a world apart from the state institution in Louisiana. "State" was the unspoken threat that loomed over everyone's head. If you don't get better, you might get sent there. Once there, you were officially crazy and given up on. You weren't going to get better. I only knew one person who was ever sent.

During visiting hours, the uneasy families would wander in, and we sat at the table performing for them. On this afternoon, we tried to catch imaginary flies with our fingers like Mr. Miyagi did with chopsticks in *The Karate Kid*. We could barely keep a straight face as visitors walked by and we'd break out in hoots and hollers after they passed.

After five weeks in the hospital, I grew weary of the restrictions, the forced medications and the locked doors, so I played the part of a model patient, and they released me for good. The final assessment on my discharge papers read:

Prognosis is probably somewhat guarded. I think she will need intensive treatment with the same therapist for a period of two to three times a week and I would say that this would have to be over a period of probably several years based on her personality organization. Psychological testing demonstrated poor reality testing and abnormal responses on the Rorschach which didn't surprise me because at times her anger got so intense she did look psychotic and I think she is at risk of developing a thought disorder at some point in the future.

I entered Berkeley a year after release from the hospital. By this time, my coping skills improved or at least morphed from self-mutilation and suicidal ideation to overeating and losing myself in relationships.

In college, I continued to seek out experiences to express my suppressed sexual energy. For a few weeks, I worked at an upscale agency in Marin County providing sensual massage. The service consisted of a real massage followed by a hand job or "release".

Marin County was known for having many houses in the exclusive enclaves of the hills that provided sensual massage; the clientele ranged from celebrities to wealthy businessmen to average men who had saved up for some special attention. I worked out of a gorgeous house with a handful of beautiful young women who all seemed to have good reasons for being there. I liked the other girls even if I didn't exactly fit in. Some had drug habits they needed to support; one girl was paying off her boyfriend's debt to the mob. I was taking first year German that semester and would do my homework in between clients.

I remember another redhead telling me, "I don't understand what you're doing here. You're smart. You could get a good paying job." I didn't know what I was doing either, but I knew I had to be there.

Victoria, the owner of the house, made it very clear in her instructions when I started: "Hand jobs only. Nothing else. I don't need us getting a reputation for giving more."

Being a good girl, I listened and followed Victoria's orders. I remember seeing other girls come out talking about their $200 tips. The biggest tip I had gotten was fifty bucks on top of the considerable amount they were paying for the massage. I wondered what I was doing wrong? Was I not desirable enough? I didn't stop to consider that I might be the *only* one following the rules.

After my first night, I pulled into the last gas station at the foot of the San Rafael Bridge right next to San Quentin prison. At 1 am, under the bright lights, I pumped gas and felt the bulge of a roll of about $300 in my jeans pocket. My mind catapulted cruel, judging thoughts about what this new job meant – about me. *What kind of woman does something like this?* The thoughts crushed me, and I felt like a woman being psychically stoned to death. I didn't have the awareness to understand that I was feeling the conditioning of others – my parents, my ancestors, my teachers, the beliefs of the world around me. When I got a slight reprieve from the internalized judgments, I actually felt good. My body felt good. I loved giving pleasure. I loved being independent. And I loved how the roll of cash felt in my back jean pocket.

I only worked there for four weeks. One night we got a phone call from another house warning us of a man who had come by on PCP and had gotten violent. They described him, his voice and the name he used and warned us not to let him in. Nothing happened, but the event sufficiently scared me. I took a few days off to go out of town for Thanksgiving with my boyfriend and never returned. I wanted to express myself and have new experiences, but not at the cost of putting my life at risk.

When I finally graduated from Berkeley, I recognized I was not ready to help other people – what a mess that would be. So I avoided my future by going home to New Orleans. I hadn't anticipated falling in love with Truth, and hadn't thought about how he would experience my hometown.

Four

I had a conflicted relationship with Louisiana and the southern culture my parents hoped I would fit nicely into. I deeply loved the South and felt a part of it in my bones, while at the same time, I despised the history, the heritage, and the lack of progress. I didn't depend on my mom and dad's approval, and for many years I wouldn't accept their emotional support. At times I consciously sought to shake them up. I hated much about "White America."

I detested the segregation of New Orleans. My parents sent me to a private school from 6th to 12th grade (the second most expensive in the city and about 98% white). It was the kind of place where you form connections that later in life help your career. Instead of appreciating and utilizing the advantages my parents went into debt to provide, I secretly despised those white benefits. I wanted to go to Ben Franklin, the magnet public school; I needed to be around different types of people, to march in Mardi Gras parades as a flag girl with the white boots with red tassels. Girls from private schools didn't march in parades.

At fifteen when I got my license, dad stretched out a map of the city on the dining room table and took a highlighter, drawing bright yellow boxes around areas of New Orleans he did not want me driving to. Do not cross the yellow lines. They could easily have been black and white lines because that's all they separated.

The lack of transparency bugged the shit out of me. Couldn't my dad just tell me, *Hey, don't drive around the projects.* But who am I to talk? I didn't say it either. Everyone understood what went unspoken. All of the "bad" neighborhoods that I shouldn't be in just happened to be black.

Dad had been an electrician for over thirty years with the utility company in New Orleans. An extremely hard worker, my dad lived for his family – his girls – my mom, sister, gram and me. From age nine to fifteen, I went to track practice six days a week with only two weeks off in August. Every single day at precisely 4:45 pm, Dad left work early to get home and take me to practice. While my friends had the ambitious corporate Dads who worked late, my Dad was the polar opposite. He would boast that he didn't have an ambitious bone in his body. If he did, perhaps he would have been a union leader, championing the rights of the working class man. People looked up to him because he always told it like it was and seemed incapable of bullshit. As the local power company got taken over by a huge corporation in the mid-nineties, he came close to losing his job at least a dozen times. He wouldn't play the corporate game of staying quiet and kissing ass. I was proud of my Dad's rebelliousness and integrity. I didn't tell him at the time. I spent most of my time being embarrassed by him because he wasn't like the other Dads. If not for my mom he'd still be wearing clothes from the sixties. He didn't care what people thought of him. Some people say they don't care but they secretly do. He *really* didn't care. He would joke with me growing up that he was physically incapable of being embarrassed. He wasn't book smart, and took unsophisticated to new heights. My mom would never try and drag him to most anything "artsy." I don't think I've ever seen him reading a novel or anything other than work manuals, the newspaper (the front section, the sports and the funnies), or his Bass fishing catalog. "I am who I am – take me or leave me," he said with his New Orleans drawl.

Growing up I idolized him, which is why it caused me such great shame, when I first heard my father use the "n" word. I cringed, as young as eleven years of age hearing him say that word. The word sounded disgusting to me, and I didn't understand why he would talk that way. They say your children will teach you the lessons you most fear learning, and Truth became one of my lessons for Dad.

Some people in Louisiana still drove around with Confederate flags on their license plates or hanging over their back window. What year are we in? What is their problem? I wanted to beep my horn, catch their attention – why are you so hateful? I imagined spitting on their car, but I did nothing.

I never had courage to spit on cars, and didn't have the conviction to communicate my feelings. Instead I escaped from New Orleans, away from the South, away from white suburban culture.

At Berkeley, I became part of the minority. Walking through Sproul Plaza and, for a split second believing I was in China or Korea, I was the odd one out. I cherished being surrounded by every race and culture imaginable. I remember wandering around the marina in San Francisco with my ex-boyfriend Joshua when in passing he called me provincial. I didn't exactly understand the connotations but I looked the word up as soon as I got home from our date, and my heart sank. I am not provincial, I proclaimed to no one but myself. Inside, I feared I had the gene, and it was white. When I wasn't looking, it might seep from my pores--the spoiled, narrow-minded white girl gene.

Before Truth arrived in New Orleans, I stood in my parents' spotless kitchen, in their 3000 square-foot, two-story white Colonial style home (in a neighborhood with a charter stating no house could be less than 2500 square feet). The house always seemed inhumanly clean to me.

Everything happened so fast with Truth, I barely told my parents anything about him. I bubbled over with the giddiness and excitement of falling in love.

"He's beautiful, and charming and smart and oh you might want to know ... he's black."

"Oh!! ... Isn't that wonderful. That is sooooo wonderful. Simply ... simply wonderful." I don't remember what my parents said, but I imagine something polite and not quite the truth. While they both carried a rebellious streak in their own unique ways, my mother set the tone of the family. Dad always backed her up. Because Mom had a terrible time dealing with her own emotional life, I learned if I'm having emotions, such as surprise, fear, anger or disappointment, just smile, lie and suck it in. Mom grew up in England and that was the way the British did things. I only knew when my Mom was upset because only during *those times* she retreated to her bedroom and locked the door. If you're going to freak out or look weak, don't show it. That was the message she ended up teaching me, though I doubt it's what she intended to pass on.

Truth never once did that to me. When he had an emotion, good or bad, it showed. At least I understood what I was dealing with.

My parents had moved into this house right around the time I left home, so I never had a room of my own. I stayed in the guest room while I waited for Truth to arrive. Then we would find a place to live together. The first night at about 10 p.m., I sat propped up in bed in the upstairs bedroom with the lamp on next to me, looking through some childhood photos I found in the bureau. Dad knocked on the door. He opened it and stood in the doorway with tears in his eyes, unable to speak. The last time I remembered seeing my father cry was when our childhood cat Tigerlily got run over by a car, and he had to go and scrape up her body.

"What's wrong Dad?"

"I don't know what to do about this ... this," he couldn't even say the word. He spoke with complete vulnerability, the kind you don't normally see in men.

He climbed into bed with me, and I held him. We both knew what *this* was. I love him for his innocence more than he could ever understand. He had no defenses; he didn't need them. I comforted him for about thirty seconds, and we didn't speak about it again. Afraid of a man he had never met? The man he probably hoped he would never have to face.

Truth arrived from Berkeley a week later, I picked him up from the Greyhound station, and we drove to Mom and Dad's home.

Truth looked forward to the challenge. He boasted that he once dated the daughter of a KKK member. As much as I reveled in being the white girl with the black man, he delighted in being the black man with the white girl. Perhaps we were destined for each other.

Mom, Dad, Truth and I all went out for dinner at Copelands, a local chain specializing in Creole and Cajun food. We sat on one side of the table holding hands and beaming every time we looked at each other. My parents would not publically question my choices, but naturally they wanted to know this man who had swept their daughter off her feet.

"Truth, where did you get your name? It's quite unusual." Mom started the polite British interrogation.

"My folks met in Berkeley in the sixties - free love and all that."

"So you grew up in Berkeley?" she continued as we gave our drink orders.

"Yes, Berkeley and Oakland, later on when my mother got remarried we moved up to Antioch, about twenty-five miles north of Berkeley."

"And what is it you *do*?" She got right to the point.

My stomach tightened as I wondered how he would answer.

"I've done a lot of things. Most recently I worked at the US Embassy in Paris."

Yes. Okay. Good choice. He told me he worked there when he was in Paris. Doing what, God only knows. I had neglected to tell my parents Truth had been married twice, most recently to a French woman. He lived in Paris two years with her and divorced before returning to Berkeley.

"Oh Paris … so you lived there?"

I'm sure this impressed Mom.

"Yes ma'am, for a few years."

"Since then I did some temporary work as a bouncer in Berkeley and I do piercings. I pierce people."

"He's also great with computers." I piped in.

My father had an engineer's mind and had played with computers since the early eighties. He began swapping hardware and software stories with Truth. By dessert Dad seemed under Truth's spell. His intellect and frenzied passion for technology dazzled my dad. He got excited when he found out Truth had served in the Army. Dad had been in the Air Force, so they bonded over shared stories of military duty.

"As long as Amy's happy, we're happy." That was my father's summation at the end of the dinner.

And that was true. But I wasn't going to make it easy on him, because I wasn't sure how deeply rooted my father's racism went. If I had ever called him a racist, which I hadn't, he would have disagreed. I remember once as a teenager hearing him say. "Well, there are black people and then there are niggers. I don't have a problem with black people."

I guess to him Truth was a black person.

Dad spent his whole life in the same five-mile radius in a city called Gretna, on the other side of the Mississippi river from New Orleans. It's the city that became embroiled in controversy when hundreds of mostly poor and black evacuees crossed the bridge trying to escape the chaos that had engulfed the Superdome in the days after Hurricane Katrina. The Gretna police set up a blockade forcing the hot, hungry and desperate survivors to turn around and return to the hell they had escaped. That's the city I grew up in.

Mom grew up in Worcestershire, a small town in England, about thirty miles southwest of Birmingham, and raised in a family that most certainly would never have a black man over to the house, but curiously, none of this wore off on her. Like my father's ignorance had not worn off on me. Intelligent and open-minded, I don't imagine Truth's race ever really bothered her. I think she probably found him as exciting as I did. "You know your father, that's just the way he is." she would say. "We love him in spite of his ways." I doubt my father ever took the opportunity to really get to know a black man, beyond the casual work related acquaintances.

We found the cheapest apartment we could stand to live in - four hundred dollars a month. One of those stately old homes in uptown New Orleans that used to be owned by a wealthy family had long since been sold and subdivided into as many one bedroom boxes as possible. Once warm and cared for, the house had been reduced to a money tree. We moved into the attic on the third floor, but the first night I discovered I was claustrophobic, so we moved down to an equally dismal unit on the second floor. From our front door you stepped right into the kitchen, about three feet wide by six feet long. You couldn't even open the refrigerator door all the way, just enough to get inside. We had to unplug the smoke detector or it would go off every time we cooked. Beyond the kitchen were two rooms, each about one hundred and fifty square feet and a long narrow bathroom.

Tiny bugs crept out of the walls; we soon discovered they were termites. They crawled everywhere. We complained numerous times, but the landlords had a key chain with about fifty different keys, and our tiny place seemed low on their list of priorities. Sawdust covered the floors in the common hallways of the building from a never-ending construction job. The paint peeled and the tiny balcony with rotting wood should have been condemned; I can't think of one likable thing about the place. But it didn't matter. We had a roof over our heads, and we were together.

We plotted our career options. We both had a lot of potential but not necessarily on the professional track. For different reasons, neither of us could tolerate working regular nine to five jobs. I was too crazy, Truth too proud. By default we became entrepreneurs.

I took a job at a yearlong Christmas shop where I'd worked before finishing college. "God Rest Ye Merry Gentlemen" 365 days a year. The paltry pay covered our rent while we started our business. Truth could do just about anything with a computer. He taught himself UNIX by buying half-dozen books, spreading them out all over our bed and reading. He would study sixteen hours a day, and within a week, he learned to program a web server. Truth never stopped working. He pushed himself harder than anyone I ever met.

He always said, "I'm a black man in America … we gotta work twice as hard as anyone else – just to get by."

He often used this phrase, "as a black man in America." Something I knew nothing about but would learn. As a black man, especially one who didn't follow the rules, Truth had a hard time. In New Orleans, a city still very much run by an old boys' network in the business sector, it was going to be nearly impossible for Truth to get ahead. He made it clear that he would not work for any white men from the South, and if a job didn't work out, he would return to France or to Berkeley.

Weeks after moving into our apartment in the summer of 1995, my parents lent us three thousand dollars to help us get set up. It bought some time to figure out what we were going to do. The surprise gift put us both in a good mood. All of my family was taken by Truth, swept away by his charm and energy. We dressed to go to a party at my sister and her roommates' house. I put my new best friend, Curtis Mayfield, into the CD player as I blow-dried my hair. I had engrossed myself in black culture, renting black movies, listening to rap, R&B, soul and funk. I liked Tupac; it was still a year before he'd be gunned down. I decided it was my responsibility to get into Truth's culture - he spent his whole life living in mine. We watched *Superfly*, and I went out and bought the soundtrack. Curtis's sweet, falsetto voice curled through the air: *I'm your pusherman.*

Truth shook his head like I committed some kind of mortal sin by singing along.

"Hey, I want you to pierce me." It was a Friday night and I felt frisky.

"Where would you like to be pierced?" he raised his eyebrow with a grin.

"NOT down there." I wasn't feeling that frisky.

"Scaredy cat."

"I prefer the phrase fear bunny. I think I'll start with my belly button."

He opened his piercing kit; I laid out on our bed watching, the sun going down from the window, still singing with Curtis. He began rubbing my pale skin with alcohol.

"I'm not gonna do this unless you stop singing."

He pulled some of the flesh above my navel with his finger and took out a few needles measuring to find the best fit

"Why do you love me?" I asked playfully. We had both used the L word in Berkeley a few weeks after we met.

He smiled rubbing his hand over my stomach. "Why do I love *mon petit tete rouge*?" His pet name for me meant *my little redhead* in French. He rummaged through his piercing kit for a hoop. "I love youuuuuuu … becauseeee" He paused pretending to not know the answer.

"Stop. *Mon petit tete rouge* is serious." I gave him a pouty look.

"Shhhh" He put his hand on my mouth. "Be still. It will only hurt for a second."

Straddling me on the bed, he pushed the needle through the fold of skin above my navel. I shut my eyes bracing for the pain not realizing he had finished. He placed a delicate kiss on my lips.

"Because you've got the kindest heart I've ever known."

I opened my eyes to see his smooth soft brown irises staring back at me.

"And your belly ain't bad either" He began licking in a circle around the ring … "and your ass … your ass … Ummmm Ummmm".

He grabbed my butt, squeezing the cheeks in his hands.

"This is no white girl booty, are you sure you didn't get mixed up in the hospital?"

We laughed as he kissed my lips. We made love with delicate care, me on my hands and knees and he behind me, so as not to touch the tender navel ring. Afterwards he picked out a bead for me, a pearl, which he attached onto the ends of the tiny hoop. He showed me how to clean the ring and care for it while healing.

He never asked me why I loved him. Perhaps he already knew. Maybe it didn't matter. It was impossible not to love him in those early days. Exotic and intoxicating like a gaseous cloud of sex and danger and adrenaline mixed in with love and a deep feeling of being protected. And terribly smart; if he had not been so smart, I would never have fallen for him. He had seen and done things in his life that some would call "bad" – but when I was in his arms, looking into his eyes I knew he was not bad. And who was I to judge? What would I have done, in his shoes? There was not a mediocre bone in his body, and that was so fucking attractive to me. With him I forgot that I had been depressed and suicidal, that I felt I didn't belong anywhere, and that I loathed myself. With Truth, I forgot myself and given my abysmal self-esteem, it felt good to be forgotten.

Five

J uly 1995 began the early stages of the biggest business revolution of our time, the Internet, and *it* was colorblind. Truth had run some Bulletin Board Systems, a primitive form of what would later become websites, so naturally he fell into learning the art of coding HTML. He decided we would start a technology company. "A tremendous opportunity" he would say. He could be the faceless figure behind an Internet conglomerate, and finally rewarded for his hard work, his talent, and his ideas. For once in his life, he wouldn't experience the racism he always knew — that was the idea.

In August, we launched Nexxus Communications, Inc. a web design, marketing and hosting business. We used my good credit to buy about ten thousand dollars worth of computer and networking equipment. We set up the computers in our apartment on two cheap white desks and went to work. Very few web design companies in New Orleans existed. Within six weeks of launching, we got a promising meeting with a prominent local bank wanting a large corporate intranet website, a lucrative potential deal. We spent two weeks doing our research and preparing to impress at the meeting. We rented an office from a lawyer for the day so we would appear more professional. We practiced delivering our proposal all morning. Truth dressed in his most business-like attire, which consisted of a sweater and the only pair of pants he owned that didn't bag. We were psyched and ready to show we knew what we were doing and could deliver exactly what they wanted.

Three white men dressed in suits walked into our faux office. They resembled the kind of men whose children I had gone to high school with, Southern, well off, old boys network. Truth wouldn't sit down at the conference table. He stood hovering. I sat them down, playing the Southern gracious host, making polite chitchat, but I could tell things were already not going well. It was just a feeling I couldn't put my finger on. I observed their faces as they scrutinized us. I could sense Truth's anxiety even as he stood behind me. I ignored the discomfort, plastering a fake smile on my face and surged forward into our rehearsed presentation: bright colored charts, mockups, tables and research about Internet security. The quiet and tenuous feeling remained in the room. Truth piped in at the right moments, explaining the technical aspects. They sat and watched us, occasionally glancing down at the plastic covered booklet. I peered over at the seersucker one and he gave me a polite, blank stare. I never experienced that look before. We weren't getting the job. While I had no tactile proof, nothing you could uphold in a courtroom or isolate in a Petri dish – it was a just a feeling. Our presentation did not matter.

After the bank meeting, Truth never showed up for a client conference in person. He groomed me to meet our customers alone. I knew how to carry myself and could be quite charming when needed. I didn't particularly want to be the face of the company, but I adjusted. I wanted our business to succeed, because if I didn't, Truth would go back to California. I didn't want to lose the man I loved, so I allowed myself to be groomed. He told me what to say, and I said it. He told me what to do, and I did it. With my fair, freckled skin and red hair, I never in my life experienced a taste of racism - as white as they come, and as naïve.

A few weeks after the presentation, we walked into a well-known computer chain, a regular occurrence, to buy equipment for our growing company. One of our hard drives crashed the night before. We browsed the boxes as a minimum wage computer geek watched us from the end of the aisle. After selecting a Western Digital drive, we walked down the next aisle to check out the scanners. There he was again following us - then on to the software aisle, and again. Truth marched up to the Customer Service counter.

"Your store is racist, and your employee is racist. You want the NAACP breathing down your neck? You damn well better show us some respect."

He threw the hard drive down on the counter.

"We've spent thousands of dollars here. If I ever catch another employee following us, I will jump over this counter and snatch you by your head and give you something to be afraid of."

The young white man appeared stunned. I followed behind, proud Truth wouldn't take shit but worried because we needed the hard drive. The door behind him slammed shut in my face. I wasn't paying attention. A memory came back of just a few months ago when my boss suggested I keep an *eye* on a few black women who entered the Christmas shop. Why had I not walked out? For Truth, this experience was old news.

In his early twenties and living in an East Bay suburb with his first wife and two young daughters, he was falsely accused of a violent crime. Someone attempted to rob a pet shop in the mall near his house; during the robbery the assailant brutally beat the older white couple who owned the store. Truth had been wheeling his youngest in a stroller through the mall; the police picked him up on suspicion of the robbery and assault. He was nowhere near the crime scene, and they had no evidence. Only the victim's testimony *"he looks exactly like the guy who beat me."* This was way before his tattoos, so they could not be used to identify him. Truth told me he started getting inked to make himself unique. He was taken to jail and released on bail. He couldn't afford a lawyer, so he used the court appointed defense attorney. Despite the lack of any physical evidence, his alibi, or testimony from numerous upstanding citizens in his town, including the local pastor, his case went to trial and into the hands of a jury - an all-white jury, as he and his family lived in a mostly white suburb. I can only imagine what he must have felt walking into the courtroom awaiting his verdict. Every single juror found him not guilty. He was exonerated and free from the charges brought against him. But not free from the pain. He could trust no one in this unfair world, including me. I had this idea in my head I could heal his pain. I would stand by his side. This was love; I believed with all my heart.

This began my re-education about this country. Now I was being followed - *presumed guilty* by virtue of my mate. Someone like me would never have these kinds of experiences alone.

I only remember being followed that one time, but we often left a shop or restaurant because Truth perceived a lack of respect. All it took was a certain look, and we split.

Sometimes, Truth's behavior frustrated me. Come on Truth; are they *all* looking at you funny? I felt like a rag doll being dragged from one place to the next in hopes of equality. I remained two steps behind him, attached by an invisible string.

Wherever he went, I went. If a white man in a store gave him a strange look, then he looked at me funny too. He would storm out. I flashed a trying-to-keep-things cool kind of smile. *It's ok. It's ok folks, nothing to see here.* I was terrified of making a scene, while Truth seemed to enjoy them.

Denial always came naturally. The sales clerk at the computer store didn't come along and say, "Excuse me, my manager told me to follow you around and make sure you don't steal anything." I remember now … Truth grabbed a box, something big, bulky and heavy like a scanner. He pounded over to the store clerk and dropped the merchandise in his arms. "If you're gonna follow us, you might as well be helpful." It's interesting I forgot that part of the story. It's really the only funny part, before he got pissed and threatened NAACP action. My cheeks flushed. Maybe you're overreacting I thought. Maybe … just maybe.

I had yet to experience *it* to my face, in the open. No one ever admits to racism except perhaps the Klan, and maybe their honesty keeps them in check because their beliefs are out in the open, so you know what you're dealing with. The bank meeting was my first time, feeling *it* happen followed by the computer store. I tried to imagine this scene happening over and over again all my life. Seeing that look repeatedly. *It* made me sad and confused.

Months later in a video store, a black woman came up to me while I perused the boxes.

"What are *you* doing with him?" She posed the question point blank, a challenge.

No one ever questioned me about us being together, not like that. I was taken aback. I must have smiled because I do when I don't know how else to act.

"Excuse me?" I asked trying to project as much attitude as I could.

She marched off as Truth walked over to me. I put my hand in his and squeezed extra tight, resisting the temptation to glance over at her to see if she saw.

Her question burned in my mind. "What are *you* doing with this man?"

I did not know, although I would never have admitted it. I unpeel the layers of my subconscious and under the first layer I find, "He's so attractive and smart and exciting." A little deeper, I find the failsafe, "I love him and he loves me – why wouldn't we be together?" or the romantic "we were destined for each other." Under all this I find a layer of curiosity, a layer of I've never had a man like him and I want to try it out. A layer of look at me I'm a bad girl. A layer of I wanna be different, of guilt, of hating my own color.

And when I cut even deeper, it gets more disgusting.

I find a memory of me as a young child of ten looking at a black girl and boy at the mall, automatically thinking I was smarter than them. I'm better. The thought crept into my head before I could stop it. I actually slapped myself in the face. Hard. Shut up Amy, what's wrong with you? Would I find a layer of *it* in there? Could I face the same racism I found so distasteful in my dad inside of me? No. I don't think so. But I knew I needed to be with Truth. I knew instinctively that he was correct for me, and whatever racial guilt or shame that lay inside of me would have a chance to heal. In those early months of our relationship, Truth and I would get into long talks about *it.*

"I didn't do those things to you or your ancestors. It disgusts me, infuriates me. You can't hold me personally accountable for what others have done."

"But, Amy, you benefit from those who did. Your life has been easy on the backs of others. How many times in your life have you gotten a break, been let in when others got shut out, received an extra hand by another white person just because you looked the same? Now imagine if you had never gotten those breaks. What if every time you were given a break, instead you were shut down, slammed in the face by the door or politely told I'm sorry we have nothing for you? And mostly done silently. How many times does it take? How many yes's turned into no's would it take to turn you into a completely different person than who you are today?"

Up until meeting Truth, I took whatever was served; so busy eating, I never once wondered if others were served equally. My life had been relatively easy with little struggle except what I had created for myself.

"I don't blame you for being white, Amy, or for having the life you've had, but we do have a problem if you choose to stay ignorant. You need to open your eyes and see that thirty years after the civil rights movement, racism, while not so direct, exists and thrives. If you sit on your pretty little butt and do nothing, then I do blame you."

Hearing his words, I slumped into my chair, my head down. I always thought of myself as basically good and loving. Now I questioned if I had been? If I closed my eyes to the injustices that affected others, was I part of the problem? How was I working towards the solution? Was just loving Truth enough?

Six

When we weren't dealing with color issues, we were completely focused on business. Any obstacle that came our way, we tackled.

It was an exciting and busy time if you ran an Internet company. Truth worked eighteen-hour days launching Nexxus. He had new programming languages to learn, graphic design skills to develop and opportunities to jump on. We plunged in headfirst. I worked at the Christmas shop to pay the bills, and Truth worked to launch the company. When I got home from my job, I would do sales and marketing. We never stopped. Seven days a week, up working until three a.m. and up by eight the next morning. We never took a day off.

Six months after launching, bits of money trickled in at the about the same speed as our leaky faucet. Truth did not like having me away at a job; it made him agitated. The stress was starting to get to us both. We had a huge poster in the office saying, "Failure is not an option." And it wasn't. We were going to succeed or die trying.

It was one of those 100-degree and 100% humidity days that New Orleans summers are infamous for; I stood on a corner in the French Quarter. Sweltering and with *We Wish you a Merry Cajun Christmas* echoing in the background, I waited for Truth to pick me up. I stiffened as I sensed a little too friendly, sketchy-looking guy approaching. I smelled the stench of alcohol on his breath. I casually started to backup into the doorway of the Christmas shop, but before I could get inside he cut me off and spit right in front of me.

"Hey Baby … I bet your pussy is juicy and red just like your hair – yeah babeeee …I bet it is … and I bet I could ram …"

Truth rolled up with the window down. Before he could get his next bet out, Truth jumped out of the car.

"Get in and drive around the corner. I'll be there in two minutes." He opened the door handing me the keys. With a calmly intense look, he turned back to the man now strutting away.

I didn't question him. I got in and slowly pulled away peering back to see what he was doing.

I saw Truth walk after the guy, stop him and begin saying something to him. I turned around the corner; I didn't want to know what would happen next. I did not enjoy conflict, either being in it or watching. I heard yelling and glass breaking. I shut my eyes and put my head down. The steering wheel was wet from my perspiration, and I now had a raging headache. I covered my ears and prayed.

Was I praying for the stranger, Truth – or myself?

Two minutes later Truth got into the car. Sweat dripped from his brow. "I don't want you working in the Quarter anymore. Too many freaks."

We never again talked about the incident. I considered the whole event a romantic gesture. I had not seen that intensity in him before. It scared me but at the same time, he was protecting me, protecting my honor. How could I not love that? I felt safe.

While Truth naturally excelled with computers, I had some kind of special power; every time I touched one, the machine broke. My parents laughed when we told them we were launching a technology company.

"But Amy, you don't know anything about computers."

Like *that* was a problem? "I don't know anything yet … it's merely a problem which time will fix."

We used my credit to finance the business, so I felt entitled to be a part it, even if I was completely unsuited for the work. I was determined to learn. We worked nonstop. With Truth's military-like discipline and tutelage, I made strides and stopped crashing hard drives. The possibility of success loomed right in front of us, but nothing was paying off.

The bills piled up from all the equipment we had financed. The meager amount of money we made from the business barely fed us. By Christmas, almost three months behind on rent, collectors began calling, so we stopped answering the phone. We would go the ATM to get money out for food, and wouldn't even have twenty dollars in the account. We'd go to the bank and get out all $13.60. This would have to last until we got our next check. Truth needed his cigarettes, so we'd buy one pack of Basics, and enough Corn Flakes, milk, bread, peanut butter and jelly to last us until our next check. When we got really hungry, we'd go to my parent's house for dinner. Too driven to be humiliated or depressed, we felt certain this was just temporary. We became experts at knowing how long we could write a rubber check before it bounced. When we used our credit card, we held our breath in unison, as the checker swiped the almost maxed Visa.

On December 26th, five months after starting our business, our landlord phoned. He was going to start eviction procedures if we did not come up with $1610 in three days. He might as well have said ten thousand dollars. Neither of us wanted to go back to my parents and ask for more money. The morning after Christmas we went to a pawnshop and sold everything of value we had. Anything we didn't absolutely need to run the business, we pawned. Every gift we received was sold. We vowed we'd buy them all back. We were a team, inseparable and completely driven no matter what the obstacles. As many teams do when they're losing and things look bleak, we began to fight.

Seven

I suppose if I had been a wiser woman looking at life with some degree of logic, I would have anticipated what would follow. Not that I could have guessed it would come from Truth because I didn't know the signs. If I was that kind of woman, I would have been ready for this. It would have seemed like a natural occurrence. Not only was I naïve and unwise, I did not like to look at my life logically.

I considered myself an optimist and trusted freely. I never even saw it coming. The last eight months had been a whirlwind of falling in love, dreaming, planning, moving in, starting our business and completely depending on each other in the midst of a tornado of stress and financial pressures barreling towards us.

I don't remember the exact day of the week, the exact time or month but I do remember the year, the season and the location. Early 1996, winter and if I had a GPS I could give you the x/y coordinates; It happened midway between my desk and the doorway of our home office in our flea infested apartment on Baronne Street.

Stressed out and disgusted with my body, I decided to go for a run – something I hadn't done since I left Berkeley. Running had always been my sure-fire stress relief since childhood. I bundled up in my purple sweatpants (the one pair that still fit with an extra fifteen pounds), a long sleeve t-shirt from a long ago road race, my grey Berkeley sweatshirt and wool hat. As I searched for my running watch I told Truth …

"I'm going for a run ok hun."

"Where?" He typed away on one of three computers at his desk.

"Along the median up St. Charles."

"At this hour?"

"It's only four o' clock" I replied.

"It'll be dark in an hour."

"And I'll be back in forty minutes – maybe thirty I'm out of shape."

"You're going out there by yourself?"

"Yeah, unless you want to come with me …"

"I'm working. Someone's got to."

"I'm just going for a run. Gimme a break."

"Yeah" he said ignoring my last comment. "When should I expect you back?"

"Sweetie, I said forty minutes." I had long since given up on finding my watch.

"Don't come complaining to me if you get raped." He was dead serious.

"What?"

"You heard me. I'll have no sympathy for you."

"Are you ok?"

"Fine" he said. I knew he was lying.

"I won't be long ok?"

I left the apartment hesitantly but started running as soon as I closed the front door. I went a half block up Napoleon to St. Charles and made a right. The streetcar clanked by with its mix of tourists and locals looking out the windows. I couldn't relax. My body ached, stiff and cold; my mind remained on Truth's words. Was he serious? Raped? How ridiculous. If it wasn't so absurd, I'd be really annoyed. I had run alone for years at all hours of the day and night in New Orleans, Berkeley, and Oakland. Never had a problem. I didn't like how it felt when he was like this. I had planned on running all the way to Audubon Park and back, about a three-mile loop, but instead turned around after running for only half a mile. I couldn't relax. I walked back into the house after only fifteen minutes upset and anxious.

"How was your run?"

"Fine." *Like he cared. It wasn't worth talking about.*

"Did you talk to anyone?"

"I was running. No."

I hadn't even built up a sweat, so instead of showering I went straight to my desk. I sensed Truth's mood was nothing to mess with. After 20 minutes of working on trying to learn how to setup tables in HTML, I looked up at my computer screen, and my eyes began to glaze over. Still early in the evening, but I felt exhausted.

"I'm gonna take a nap. I'm beat."

With that, something snapped inside of him. He didn't say anything, just got up and went into the bedroom and began to pace.

Ok … so I guess a nap is a bad idea.

A few minutes later he came into the office. His eyes normally a beautiful deep brown, appeared darker.

"Who do you think I am?" he asked still pacing.

"Truth … I'm tired."

"What do you think *I* am?"

"Then let's go to bed early – together." I got up from my desk chair and walked over to him, hoping to appeal to some other side of his mood. He turned away.

"Who exactly is going to be in here? How exactly do you think this company is going to take off if we take early nights? Go ahead, Amy. Go ahead and go to sleep if that's what you want. I have to work."

"Fine." I was tired of everything – tired of him, tired of the office, tired of my computer and I needed to feel the softness of our bed under my body. I needed to disappear under the covers. I couldn't hold on any longer. "Ok then – I'm going to bed. I'm sorry. I'll catch up tomorrow."

"Fine."

Without even changing my clothes or brushing my teeth, I got into bed, brought the comforter over me and closed my eyes. Minutes later he flipped on the switch towering over the bed.

"Am I your boy? Is that it? You think I'm your boy?"

"Truth ... no ... I don't ... I just need to sleep. I can't work every day anymore." He pulled off the covers. My instincts told me to move out of the way fast. I jumped up and walked into the office over to my desk - a seemingly safe harbor.

He charged into the office and punched me in the face. As his fist hit my cheek, I fell over into my chair. I was in shock. I said nothing. *You didn't just* ... I don't remember if it hurt. I think it did.

It never occurred to me something like this would ever happen. How strange. I could pinpoint on a map of the universal continuum - the first time I was smushed like a grape but I refused to see it coming. Refused to put two and two together and anticipate this day. I really didn't believe it had just happened. I was a straight A student, graduated with honors. I had a million options at my doorstep. I took Women's Studies at Berkeley, for God sakes, which must count for something. I wanted to laugh at him. I wanted him to laugh with me. I wanted to fall over with belly laughs on the bed ... "Truth, you didn't just hit me" I would say with a giggle. "Your hand didn't just fly across space and time and meet my face and knock me to the chair." I would barely get the word chair out because I'd be grinning so hard. *This is a joke, right?* I honestly thought it was an accident. I'm not stupid. I just didn't want to believe. It was not in my cards to be here in this space and time with this man facing this. But there I was.

I sat in the chair touching my face. He walked back into the bedroom still pacing, mumbling under his breath. He turned and walked back in the office right up to me. My body instinctively turned inward, my head down, my arms folded in covering my face and my torso bent, like the petals of a blossoming flower in reverse.

"What is your problem? Shit! Please stop crying."

I said nothing. Couldn't say anything. Even if I could, I knew better than to say a thing. This wasn't the Truth I knew. I had no idea who this man was before me.

Eight

We never discussed what happened. I decided the punch was a strange cosmic mishap, a meteor falling in my front yard. Work took my mind off the fight. After about ten months of eighteen hour, seven-day workweeks, we started to make some money. In fact, the dollar bills began to pour in. Over the course of one day, with one new client, everything changed.

"Truth, I just got off the phone with Gary. He's sending a potential customer our way. He wants twenty websites!"

We had been having discussions with Gary, the owner of our hosting company, about collaborating on a large search engine project. It would be called Pandoran. Truth would be taking the lead on coding and they would handle equipment and bandwidth. The project consumed much of his time, but would pay us nothing for a while.

"You're kidding ... Why don't you call him right now."

"He does porn sites."

His fingertips kept punching away at his computer, typing only with his index fingers but at break-neck speed. He'd burn through a new keyboard every three months.

"Yeah?" He continued battering away at the keys. "Can we afford to care about this?"

"Not really." I did the books, paid what little of the bills I could. I knew we couldn't afford to care about who we took on as clients. Two weeks before I had filed for chapter thirteen bank-ruptcy. All my credit cards had defaulted, and our attorney advised us to file or expect the creditors to come after the business equipment. Twenty websites at roughly a thousand dollars a site would pay our back rent and past due bills as well as leaving some money to move the hell out of this dump, and we'd still have money in the bank. At the moment, we were lucky to bring in eight or nine hundred a month. Our clients, mostly small compa-nies who didn't understand the power of the web, did not want to invest a lot into something new. We still had a few years until the mainstream business community would truly embrace e-commerce.

It was no surprise to anyone working on the web that porn made money. In those days, porn was the only thing making money. We're talking before Amazon, Google and EBay; Mark Zuckerberg was still in middle school. Hundreds of millions came from the sex industry and drove the Internet in the early and mid-nineties. It paid for the servers, the bandwidth and new technolo-gies. Good old fashioned fucking. Programmers, heads of business development, CEOs and designers all found themselves in the same position: Do we embrace this? How the hell could we not?

"I'm calling … I'm calling."

Jeremy, our new client, barely out of high school, had jumped on the bandwagon early. Jeremy excelled in marketing - aggressive marketing. We struck a deal. We would design twenty small websites at five hundred dollars each; in return for the discount he would teach me how to make money by driving traffic to adult websites.

Every night Truth worked on the sites, and I called Jeremy to chat. Jeremy was Jewish and in love with Alanis Morrisette. Her "Jagged Little Pill" was going down quite smoothly with him. I liked her as well, and we usually started our talks gushing about our mutual love for Alanis.

He could have been selling toilet paper; it made no difference to Jeremy that he sold bodies – breasts and legs and hair and vaginas. He appeared to have no emotional attachment to the content, nor did he seem to get aroused. Numbers turned Jeremy on, and numbers were what he taught me. His porn income paid his way through one of the top law schools on the East Coast.

We embarked on our adult entertainment enterprise, and I found myself profoundly interested in the female bodies we sold and profoundly guilt-stricken with the act of selling them. Make money or feel guilty – doing both is stupid and counter-productive. But, my life was all about being stupid and counter-productive. I spent hours looking at their perfect forms that appeared without scratches, without bruises, without cuts, without cellulite, without a hint of imperfection – God's finest creations. Who could be unhappy looking at such gorgeous women? I could almost see the delicate hands of angels sculpting their curves.

The deal turned out very well for us. After my training period ended, and Truth began designing our own porn sites, the money started to roll in. We began marketing phone sex numbers and live video shows from Canada and Amsterdam. If you remember what video looked like in 1995 on the web, you saw a grainy, pixilated image, followed by another image a second later, and then another image three seconds later; the screen looked like the flipbooks you'd make as a child, except instead of a flower growing or bird flying you had live naked women gyrating and touching themselves as men logged in from the privacy of their own home to ogle them. These men paid up to six bucks a minute to talk to these naked girls. The videos sold like hotcakes to starving bands of burly lumberjacks.

We got our first report back from the company that produced the shows. They faxed us a daily spreadsheet with the amount of minutes we sold the day before. We would be paid two dollars a minute. We waited anxiously in front of the fax machine and couldn't believe our eyes when we read the smudged black ink text on the thermal paper roll out. $743. $743? $743. For one day.

We embraced in front of the machine with the torn fax page clutched in Truth's hand. The financial stress made us distant. We reunited like old lovers, feeling profound relief as the desperation started to lift from our shoulders simultaneously. Our dire future appeared suddenly brighter. I felt safe in his arms as he stroked my hair. Truth pulled away from the hug first. He looked over at the image on my computer of a beautiful brunette with pouty lips and perfect C cup breasts with her tan legs spread wide as she touched herself.

"So this is what we're doing. Porn?" I wasn't sure if it was a statement or a question and a hint of embarrassment clung to his voice. Like I should say, "No ... no honey we're better than this. We can succeed as real designers." I don't think I had ever seen him embarrassed before.

"Yeah, looks like this is what we're doing." I wasn't embarrassed. In the back of my head, this is exactly the kind of thing I thought I would end up doing. It fit perfectly with my secret belief that I was a bad girl – a bad seed even – and we all know under the right conditions, bad seeds sprout into pornographers.

Contrary to popular notions, Porn is not all about fake body parts and blonde hair. Porn was also, for me, not all about fucking. I didn't even particularly like the fucking – boring and monotonous. I noticed it on the women's faces (the ones who were either new and didn't know how to fake it or too weary to fake it). They were bored too. For me, it was about beautiful bodies and the women who possessed them – bodies that did not feel the shame that I did. Proud bodies, happy, perfectly at one with themselves and their place in the world – namely, they ruled it. I looked at my body, getting fatter and fatter, in all its imperfections and their flawless limbs and stomachs and breasts, and I loved them. I wanted to be them as I naively imagined they had perfect lives to go with their perfect figures. Their bodies paid our bills. I worked as the middleman or woman sandwiched in between God's perfection and his sins.

At any given time, we always kept one "straight" client – bakeries, clothing boutiques, accountants, whatever we could drum up – just so we could pass ourselves off as web designers, not pornographers, and still be telling the truth.

First we moved out of the slum and into an elegant two-bedroom apartment in uptown New Orleans. Our 1200 square foot freshly remodeled space had no termites. It took up one half of the upstairs of a huge peach Victorian house on Prytania Street a few blocks from the neighborhood theatre. It was another one of those stately old New Orleans homes, but well cared for. The owner lived downstairs so he maintained the house in top shape. Next we drove back to the pawnshop where we'd stashed our valuables. We bought everything we'd sold on our earlier day-after-Christmas visit; surprisingly we found every item there except for my camera. Truth went out and bought me the top of the line Nikon SLR camera. We basked in relief and satisfaction knowing our business was going to make it. While the money started to flow from porn, we didn't get lazy. We worked harder and longer hours. So much money to make and so many bodies to sell. When we weren't working, we treated ourselves and tried to ignore the dangerous dynamic developing between us. Whenever stress got to be too much, we'd spend more money.

Neither of us drank much. We didn't do drugs so shopping became our outlet. We also ate. Or I should say, I ate. And ate and ate and ate. Over the first year of our living together, I gained nearly fifty pounds.

I had a long history of weight fluctuations but because of my running, I had kept huge weight gain at bay. The fat cells shrouded in the corner always just waiting to be plumped up again. I grew up with a taste for sugar and fast food. Long ago I started connecting eating rich food with pleasure. When I felt bad or sad or mad – all the "ad" words drove me straight to the fridge. We had no time for good nutrition; we lived on the self-styled Internet Startup Diet: lots of take out, pizza and soda. Truth put on weight as well but not nearly as much as I did.

I didn't acknowledge the true extent of the weight gain, until a trip one day to Mackenzie's Bakery. Mackenzie's had the best glazed donuts in New Orleans, a well-known fact. Freshly baked and when you warmed them up with the sugar dripping off, it was heaven for someone with a sweet tooth. All of the MacKenzie stores hired at least one developmentally disabled person as a matter of policy. At the store on Prytania a young girl with short brown hair worked the weekday shift. It had been about ten weeks since our last visit.

"You got fat," she said to me as she walked out from the kitchen with flour on her stubby little hands. Not "Hello," or "Haven't seen you for a while." Just "You got fat."

"Well you're retarded," I wanted to retort. But of course she was right and the only person willing to tell me the truth.

I let the excitement of the business taking off and the money coming in serve as distractions. Fat maybe, but at least I would be fat and rich. I could afford some exercise equipment. Things were both very good and very bad, and mostly, they were beginning to spin out of control.

The money continued to pour in, and averaged twenty-five to thirty grand a month. Ten to fifteen of that became expendable income. I couldn't tell you where we spent it all. We received supreme pleasure from walking into a store and feeling like we could buy just about anything.

We invested a lot of the money back into the company with new equipment. We bought lots of toys for ourselves. We purchased all of the latest high tech gadgets and usually more than one: the latest TVs, cameras, video cameras, surround sound stereos. Two grand for two mountain bikes I don't even think we road twice. We obtained every single appliance known to man. Not that we needed them as Domino's doesn't need to be Cusinarted or charbroiled on our Williams and Sonoma Stovetop Grill.

And we bought guns – Truth's idea, but it wasn't out of the realm of possibility for me. We lived in New Orleans after all – a city that in those years held the highest murder per capita rate title in the United States. My father and sister both had firearms. We entered the Gretna gun shop, and Truth told me to pick out any one I wanted. I picked out the cutest one. I cared more about firearm fashion then utility. I held the small, black automatic Colt pistol in my hands and aimed at the wall. The salesman cautioned it might not be effective against some assailants because of its size. One bullet or even two might not stop them. I didn't care. I liked it. We purchased it – $460. Truth bought a large automatic Ruger, a long hunting rifle and his favorite – a shotgun with a short pistol grip. Legal in Louisiana, they classified it as an assault rifle and outlawed it in California.

"Only one thing this gun is good for – killing people." Rather than a judgment, the gun salesman said this with pride with his deep drawl as he held it up to show Truth.

"I'll take it," he said.

Or did he say, "We'll take it." I can't remember.

We also spent money on transportation – specifically limousines. The first time it was a joke. A novelty. We decided to go out and celebrate our business success.

"Let's take your parents out to dinner." Truth suggested. "Let's rent a limo and surprise them."

"A limo? A bit much, don't you think?"

"No, they'll love it. We're celebrating."

Reluctantly I called the limo company and ordered the car to come pick us up. People ordered limos for proms or weddings or movie premieres, none of which applied. I watched the shiny black car with tinted windows pull up in front of our house, and my stomach began to cramp up which might have been from the fried food I had at lunch or maybe because just months ago we battled termites and collectors; a limo didn't seem like the best use of our money. I did like the idea of surprising my parents. Hell, you only live once. So I went along. I wanted my parents to be proud of me, to be proud of us. We're doing ok Mom ... we're doing more than ok. Look can't you see? We're doing 20-foot stretch limo kind of ok. And my parents, who knew about our porn business, seemed impressed. My mom, especially, being a CPA, lived in the world of numbers and profit and loss statements and money equating to a good life – by all appearances, we certainly lived a good life.

Truth was right. The first two or three times I had a great time in the limos. The stares we got when getting out. I think people thought Truth was some sort of Rap star. Maybe that's what he secretly wanted to be. He developed an insatiable taste for being driven around in long shiny cars; Truth wanted to order a limo every time we went out. We actually had a *regular* driver. The car company knew to send us a black car. One time they made the mistake of delivering a white one because all the black vehicles were out. "Go tell them to send it back and bring us a black one," he said after peering through the curtains down to the street. It got to a point where we didn't even have to be going out anywhere special. If we had dinner plans, errands even, and were going to be out for their minimum of three hours, we took a limo. We drove to Sam's Wholesale Club for water and cat litter in a limo and to Office Depot to pick up some ink cartridges in a limo. I began to despise them – everything about the overstretched body scream-ing for attention, the smell of the leather seats that deserved more bodies to enjoy them, the bar that was impossible to mix a drink in without spilling, the tiny TV that we never watched because we had big ones at home and the telephone that wasn't needed since we both had cell phones. And the driver, I hated the driver the most because he saw (if he ever looked back) that no celebrating ever went on in our limos.

I was paying back the money from the bankruptcy. Of course filing had ruined my credit, which never bothered me because I could afford to lead a luxurious lifestyle on cash. I didn't have a savings account, or retirement account. It wasn't that I didn't want to save money. We kept saying we'd save some money – just not yet.

Nine

In a recurring dream I have, I stand in the backyard and see a whole line of tornadoes coming directly towards us, one after another. I frantically warned my family to run, but they did not take my advice.

A real tornado never hit me, but when Truth got upset that's what it felt like. With very little warning, from nowhere, a loud train-like sound came toward me. Sometimes I would make it to the bathroom to hide before it hit, sometimes I didn't. Wham. The shutters would be ripped from the siding, doors from their nails; the kitchen sink would end up in the closet. By the fourth tornado, I finally admitted to myself I had a problem. Even a hardheaded girl like me couldn't deny four tornadoes hitting the same person was too much for coincidence, and could not be called an accident. I also realized it would not stop.

About a year after the first time I remember searching online for 'Battered Wife' and from the results I discovered that our relationship fit all the criteria. I had studied all of this at Berkeley; I knew all about the Cycle of Abuse and the Wheel of Power and Control, but I compartmentalized it. *This is what happens to other women. This is not what is happening to me.* Our relationship could have been the example in the textbook: The quick commitment, subtle then not so subtle control, possessiveness and extreme jealousy, followed by build-up where I'd walk on eggshells, then the explosive violence. Following the tornado, the humanitarian groups would roll in to help with the cleanup. Truth would come to me with his heart-felt apologies, little gifts and promises that it would never happen again. So unoriginal, it wasn't even funny.

After the night I went out to run and the first attack, I never went out into the world without Truth. Never. I could have. He didn't say not to – at least not verbally. But based on the few times I tried to go out when he didn't want me to, I learned quickly it was a fast track to his rage. Like many abusive men, Truth believed I wanted to fuck every male out there, and if out on my own, I would do just that. He suspected I was an insane fucking machine on overdrive. I never desired another man – not once the whole time. Desire takes energy, and I had none.

As the pounds piled on, my self-esteem plummeted. Eventually, I stopped making eye contact with anyone – man or woman. Not that this mattered. One evening at Winn Dixie, we walked through the frozen foods section when Truth started in on me.

"So who is he? Who the fuck is he? You gonna start this shit with me tonight? Who the fuck is he?" He went off walking ahead of the grocery basket and me.

"What are you talking about?" I knew where this was headed but sometimes my curiosity got the best of me: I wanted to know who he thought caught my eye.

Truth was one of only three people that I had ever told about my massage job in Marin County. In a moment of intimacy, I wanted him to know everything about me, so I shared the story with him.

"I never had sex with any of them. I know how it looks but that's the truth."

I'm quite sure he never believed me.

"Don't fucking lie to me. I saw you smile at him. Don't lie to me. You want him. Is that it? He turns you on. Fuck this, he can have you, I'm through with you!" and he stormed out of the store.

He left me next to the Sara Lee pound cakes. Convenient. This is a joke, right? What the hell was he going on about? I had no earthly idea what guy he was even talking about. This script read worse than a bad soap opera. I picked up the pound cake, reading the back, pretending to care about the calories and tossed it into the basket. I took my time walking to the checkout dreading the rage I'd face when I got to the car.

I could usually tell where he resided on the temper scale. Every morning I instinctively learned to take his emotional temperature, learn what I had in store for myself for the day. *Today ladies and gentlemen we have blue skies and a calm, upbeat Truth.* On the more stressful days, *today I would keep my distance … dark clouds and possible dangerous lightning and twisters. Get into the bunker and protect yourself.* On those days when I knew something was up, I stayed at least ten feet away and offered lots of appeasement. Be good and be helpful and don't give him any reason to get upset. In reality, when he was ready to explode, I could do nothing to stop him. Sometimes, like in Winn Dixie, his fuse blew instantly. All logic flew out of the window.

Why did I stay? I used to yell to the women on Oprah, *Why would you stay?* I had options. I had a family who loved me, who would take care of me if I left. I wasn't married to him nor did we have children together. The only tie we had was the business, and on paper we owned it fifty/fifty. *Why put up with this? What is wrong with you?*

I don't have a good answer. Not a logical one, only emotional answers. When I fell in love with him, I fell too far to get out on my own. Maybe this was the "has difficulty functioning in a way society accepts as normal" part of my borderline personality. I saw the abusive Truth as an imposter, and the real Truth, the one I loved, was locked somewhere inside. If I tried hard enough, loved deeply enough, I could find him. I might even say – rescue him. As my self-esteem began to shatter, it became impossible to put me back together, and shattered young women do not make the best rescuers. When Truth exploded, along with the hitting, he threatened me with much worse actions if I didn't stay in line. "I'll kill you; I'll kill your entire family." The threats felt even more painful than when he laid hands on me; eventually the physical abuse came only in spurts – maybe once or twice one month then no flair ups for a few months. He had learned how to control me without it – just a look would be enough.

During the abuse, I split myself into many different parts. Time stretched and molded to fit my needs. The tiniest expression of love or moment of joy – a good night – expanded like a rubber band into a whole month. The moments of greatest fear and terror collapsed into a blink of the eye. I became author of my own fictional tale. I used my imagination to create a portrait of a livable life. If you keep your eyes closed and your mouth shut, you can exist forever in that state. If you saw me on the street and asked how I was doing. I would smile and say fine. *I'm doing just fine.* If you weren't really paying attention, you would believe me.

Sometimes during our worst fights, everything seemed to happen in slow motion, and an orchestral score played in the background. The strings increased in intensity as I retreated away from him, the beating of the percussions as he followed me, the flutes as I tried to calm him, as his hands met my body, the crescendo hit with symbols clapping together at the finale of a symphony. I heard the music we listened to in my dreams as two cultured, mature adults in love and enjoying the arts. As I reached up to my face or back or stomach or chest to feel the damage, I heard the audience applauding, jumping to their feet with a standing ovation. Bravo! Bravo! Tears started to pour out of me, and the rest of the audience, inspired by the music. The show had ended, and as the sophisticated, art-appreciating couples walked to their cars to begin talking about how the music reminded them of this or that, Truth came to me and apologized. He didn't mean for it to go this far. His most vulnerable expressions to me came directly after his explosions. How everything felt wrong. How he shouldn't let stress do this to him. How it would never happen again.

I probably said *if this happens one more time I'm leaving* about fifteen times. About fifteen times, I made threats to him and promises to myself I never kept. The thought of escaping certainly occurred to me. That's about as far as it could go. I couldn't locate my self-esteem. I gained about seventy-five pounds. I was dying inside, suffocating, losing all sense of my self and my power.

I felt like a beached whale abandoned on a desert island with not a marine biologist in sight to rescue me. I took myself there. I had a lot of feelings about it, but none of them pointed in the direction of freedom. A hallmark of the abused woman dwelling in isolation, I didn't stay in touch with any of my friends, after Truth and I moved in together. No girlfriends, no role models, no teachers – no faith, just a few fibers of thin thread holding me together. I thought about the kitten in the poster I saw as a child; holding on to a rope and the caption read something like, "When life is rough, tie a knot and hold on." So I stuffed more food down my throat and tried like hell to hang on to my knot.

When the pain became too much, I regressed back to cutting. I had only cut a handful of times since I met Truth. Our life together did not leave spare time for self-indulgent habits.

I curled up in the corner of the bathroom one afternoon. I don't remember the exact nature of the drama but I expect either a) being in love with a man who hit me. b) not being able to stop eating. c) not telling anyone what was going on. d) not being able to leave, or most likely e) all of the above.

With my knees pulled tightly to my chest I rocked back and forth, the razor blade lying next to me still waiting to cut into my flesh. I had perfected a very precise, clinical cutting ritual producing just the right amount of blood, enough to release what I couldn't say with words. I cried trying to sooth myself, trying to stop myself. I knew enough by now to understand cutting didn't fix anything. It had been months since I last got to this place.

Truth appeared at the door. He had been watching me a few minutes but in my self-absorption I had not noticed. He looked at me with a mixture of confusion, contempt and a hint of fear.

"What are you doing?" he said his voice rising.

I stared up at him pleading with my eyes for some warmth and understanding or even sympathy.

"Nothing." I looked down. This was my private ritual, and not something I shared with anyone even though this time I left the door unlocked.

"I thought you were done with that poor little white girl stupidity."

I showed him my white arms with not a hint of blood, only the long ago faded scars of past bad days, which had nothing to do with him. Somewhat proud I had not given in to the urge, although if he had walked in two minutes later I'm not so sure I could have said this. "I am through, see? I just feel comforted by it." The stainless steel blade lay on the floor next to me.

"That's really sad Amy ... incredibly pathetic." He walked over to me and with his huge arms he scooped me up and placed me down on the toilet seat.

"What are you doing?"

He picked up the blade and grabbing the alcohol from the closet, he drenched the metal.

"What the fuck are you doing, Truth?"

"You want to cut yourself? You really want to cut yourself – to kill yourself? I'm gonna show you how to do it correctly."

He grabbed my hand and held it on top of the washbasin.

"Stop ... this isn't funny. Let go ... you're hurting my arm."

"No. You want to play with your life like this. I'm gonna show you how to do it right. You see this?" He pointed to my old scars. "You did this shit all wrong – wimpy – you want to do it right, you need to cut vertically." He pointed the tip of the blade onto my flesh and without drawing blood dragged vertically. "Right along the vein."

I didn't know how far he would go. His dark brown eyes appeared impenetrable.

"Are you ready to die?"

Our eyes locked on each other. I could feel his breath on my face. He didn't blink and he didn't take the blade off my wrist.

"Didn't your mother ever teach you that if you do something, you should do it right?" He sneered at me.

Tears began rolling down my face. "Please, please stop. Just stop."

"White girls."

He released my arm and walked out of the bathroom. I sat frozen on the toilet, alone with my stupid white girl wimpy feelings. I threw the blade and the box with the rest of the blades into the trash, blew out all the white snot from my nose, wiped all the clear white tears from my face, walked out the bathroom and went back to work.

Ten

In early 1998, we moved back to the Bay Area. Money gave us options and we decided we had our fill of the Deep South. I tried to be hopeful; a change of scenery might improve our situation. We flew to San Francisco and stayed at the St. Francis, a posh hotel in Union Square, while searching for a new home. We found a place online and fell in love with it. An architect designed and built the house by hand. It stood the very last house at the top of a hill just north of Berkeley on the edge of a huge state park called Wildcat Canyon. A home design magazine had featured the house in one of its spreads because it resembled a lighthouse. The large entryway had a circular shape that shot up 3 stories and from a distance it had the look of a lighthouse. The architect loved sailing; he and his wife planned to rent their house and sail around the world. We both wanted it but had one problem: we knew we'd never get in if they ran a credit check. They already faxed us the application requiring our credit information.

"I really love this house, Truth."

"We're going to get it. Listen, this will work. First, we rent a car."

By car he meant limo, of course.

"We tell them we're coming from an important business meeting – hence the car. We bring them bank statements, tax returns and have a check already written for the first, last and deposit. We'll say we need an answer today."

"I hate lying."

"Who said anything about lying? We can easily afford the place."

"Yeah, I know that. You do all the talking, ok?"

"No. No, that's not a good idea. We don't know what kind of people they are. I'll be in the car. You go by yourself. Tell them I flew out of town right after the meeting."

I looked at him with a pleading expression, begging him to come with me. He put his hand over mine.

"You can do this."

We weren't coming from a meeting. We didn't need a limo, and Truth was not flying out of town. Even though every molecule in my body screamed that I hate being dishonest, I had learned how to handle myself, and I had learned how to lie quite convincingly. I took a deep breath, grabbed our documents and walked out to impress the architect and his wife while Truth looked on from behind the darkened window of the limousine.

It worked. As we drove to the hotel to celebrate, thrilled with the prospect of living in the beautiful lighthouse – excited about our new life back in California, sadness clung to me. Truth assumed we wouldn't get the house if they saw him. He just might be right. Keeping my melancholy to myself, I held his hand and smiled in our shared success.

We packed up our Prytania apartment. Two years ago, we only had a suitcase and a few boxes each. Now we could barely fit all of our possessions into a twenty-four foot Ryder Truck. Dad joined; we drove cross-country – back home for Truth – and this time in style.

"Take care of my girl." Dad said after he had helped us safely arrive.

After two days of non-stop unpacking, we got to work. The house had a separate studio area about fifteen yards from the main house with two attached offices. We installed a T1 line into the garage to run our servers. Truth worked as driven as ever but seemed more relaxed now back in California with his family nearby. We threw a big party at the house and invited his whole family. His sister Barbara, cousin Roger, Grandma Ellis on his mom's side, his grandma on his dad's side and his aunties, Diana, Louise and Robin and countless other distant cousins and nephews and nieces – I met them all. They accepted me with open arms. Impressed with our success, I must be good for Truth, they said.

Eighty percent of our time we spent working. In the remaining hours we slept, ate, fought, shopped and occasionally fucked – not necessarily in that order. We stood together in shared pride of how hard we had worked to make our business successful. Truth handled all the programming, server maintenance and design, and I was in charge of sales, marketing and office administration. I worked my ass off and became very good at marketing porn sites. In fact, I soared to the top of the field for a while.

Concerned for my privacy and security; Truth decided I'd use an alias for all porn related work. I came up with two as it made our company seem bigger. Pat Anderson became the main one, and she was sharp, aggressive and a highly capable businesswoman. You didn't mess with Pat. She could shoot the shit with the boys, but would be the first to call you on it if you tried to take advantage of her. In the online porn business, with its Wild West mentality, people constantly tried to cheat us out of money. We worked as affiliates for many large companies; we would advertise their adult online services and they would send us large checks based on our signups. There were more than a few occasions when companies would go bankrupt after CEOs stole all the money and left for the Caymans. Pat had an incredible knack for sensing when such fiascos were about to occur and on two occasions saved us over forty thousand by redirecting our traffic to other programs just before the companies went under. Pat was good at it knowing when to leave. Amy, on the other hand, was not.

I chose the name, Pat because on paper, she could be a man or woman, and in this business that helped. I chose Anderson because it was the last name of beautiful girl I once knew. My second alias became Kara Sears, and she was lighter and more flirtatious on the phone. When I needed to use my feminine wiles, Kara took over. In my imaginary alias world, Kara Sears worked as Pat Anderson's assistant and in real life had been my pen pal and one of my few very close girlfriends as a child. We became best friends in first grade, then she moved the next year; we wrote to each other for over ten years as her family moved from state to state. I lost touch with her at eighteen, and I liked being reminded of her.

We employed other people on larger projects, but remained the pair at the helm of central porn command. After two years of always feeling like I messed things up, I finally began holding my own professionally. We had big dreams of buying a house, retiring early. Anything was possible in the late nineties with the Internet boom. We would have weekly planning meetings, where Truth would sketch ideas that usually amounted to some sort of plan for world domination within our market niche.

Truth always carried out plans in a hurry. Whatever needed to be done, it always needed to be done now. He would get an idea for something and we'd have to go out at 9:45 PM rushing to get to the store to buy new equipment for his plans. It was always like that. We never waited to do anything. One of our big sources of argument was that even after we started to make a huge profit, he still worked sixteen-hour days, and I didn't want to. If Truth ever worked for a Microsoft or Apple, I expect there would have been no limits to his success. But he would never work for anyone else. I was the other half of his company, and I did not have his drive. He resented working more hours than I worked, and I refused to work myself into sickness. I managed, on a few occasions, to get him to take a break, but mostly he would not listen to me.

I stood peering out of the window from our new lighthouse. I observed rolling hills, nibbling deer, grazing cows and picturesque greenness. I had never lived in a house with such a breathtaking view. I never imagined I would be able to afford such a beautiful house.

I remember how I felt gazing out from the tiny bathroom window of our termite-infested slum. I remember looking out of the kitchen window of our nice two bedrooms uptown home in New Orleans, and how I felt. Now I gazed out from our redwood deck over miles of green hills – as far as the eye could see lay natural beauty, and I remember how I felt.

The same.

Exactly the same in all three homes.

Lost, out of control and wishing for a different life. It would be wrong to say it wasn't nicer to have money and be lost. It was. But lost was still lost. Assuming you really wanted to be found. And I don't think I wanted to be found. The irony of the lost living in a lighthouse never ceases to make me smile.

Eleven

We had been living together for three years. Despite our problems, we remained faithful to each other; our shared hell had no time for other partners. I am pretty certain he never cheated on me, mainly because we were never separated long enough.

The corporate papers listed us as full partners with equal shares of the business. We had no reason to get married, except that we just finished watching *Fools Rush In*, a sweet, romantic comedy about an interracial couple who have a one night stand in Las Vegas and fell in love. We needed a break from work, so on a Friday night in February of 1998 we flew to Vegas and got hitched. We decided at about 8 pm. The last plane to Vegas departed at 9:45 pm. I called my mom at about 8:15 pm after I jumped out of the shower. I can only imagine what she thought. Well as long as you're happy. I think that's what she said. *Happy.* I felt excited. My life never felt dull. But happy? No, not happy.

We arrived at the 24-hour chapel at about one am. At this late hour, they had to page the officiant to come out and perform the service. He told us he worked a second job as an embalmer at the county morgue, and he had been working there when he got the call. As we watched the ceremony of a couple from Sweden, my mind wondered back to my little girl fantasies about my wedding day.

Childishly, I assumed one day a man would come for me. He would knock on the door of my childhood home; my parents would answer; he'd walk in and SWOOP me off the blue slate floor of our foyer. Or was it WOOSH? One of those, and I'd be off my feet and in his arms. Next, we'd get married. He didn't have a horse in my dreams. He walked, still carrying me, to the church. I wore a beautiful white, satin dress, big and poofy, and he gently placed me down at the front door of the chapel. Now, it got tricky. I had this fear; I actually stayed up nights mulling it over-- how would I know when to walk down the aisle? The man stood there next to the priest, all the guests sat in the pews, and I stood frozen at the top of the aisle. How would I know when to start walking? It bothered me to no end. I don't think music existed in this dream. Then POOF all my childish thoughts disappeared as they do.

I found myself waiting at the top of a very short aisle in a small room with low popcorned ceilings, no guests, and Truth, with a part-time embalmer, standing ahead of me. I took a deep breath and walked. *I* decided when to walk. That's how it worked. This was not what I had dreamed of. But I didn't doubt for one minute that I wanted to marry Truth. My life turned out so far beyond what I had imagined it would be; who was I to argue? I wanted to be married, and getting married might change things. We said our, *I do's*, kissed, and it was done. We posed for pictures on their tacky, fake Bridge of Love. A week later I would go to develop the film, but every picture came out of the processing machine blank.

Getting married made us serious about fixing our relationship problems. It made us start talking about a future – having a good life together, having kids one day. We made some appointments with a therapist to deal with things. We made three appointments. Or should I say, I made three appointments, specifically with a black therapist so Truth would feel comfortable. Three appointments we found a reason not to keep.

In April of 1999, fifteen months after leaving New Orleans, we moved to Las Vegas. It was the fastest growing city in America and the location of many businesses in adult entertainment. We'd be able to buy a house in Vegas much quicker than in the Bay area. We looked for a place to rent, while we got ready to buy. We found a four thousand square foot house on Cathedral Canyon Court in northern Las Vegas. It was a beautiful new suburban house – fresh, clean and looked much like every other house on the block. This time we didn't use limousines; Truth came with me to meet the realtor and see the house.

The house opened to a foyer and large formal living room; a few steps up to the formal dining room. The ceilings rose vaulted about 20 feet and the upstairs hallway looked down onto this area. We walked into a huge open floor plan kitchen and family room with tan carpet, white grooved tile walls, wet bar and fireplace. Standing in the sparkly kitchen, I noticed what looked like a dried bloodstain in one of the cabinets – about the size of a dinner plate in an elliptical shape. I whispered to Truth to look at it, being too embarrassed to bring it up in front of the real estate agent. What is that? Maybe someone died in the house we whispered to each other.

Downstairs housed two bedrooms, a laundry room and three-car garage. Upstairs we found four more bedrooms, including a huge master with walk in closet and large bathroom with whirlpool tub. The master bedroom had rose-colored carpet and a flower patterned wallpaper neither of us liked. We used three of the upstairs bedrooms for offices; one had hardwood floors, which Truth immediately claimed as his. "First dibs" he said before I even got up there to see it. I didn't care; I had my own separate space to work in without him breathing down my neck.

We started fresh – a clean slate in a new house in a new town. Moving gave us energy like a new year that we hadn't yet fucked up. We explored Las Vegas together. We were going to turn things around. We both wanted to get healthy – healthy bodies and healthy minds. We planned to buy a house and start our family. We talked about the future, which was a new thing. So much of our life so far had been just surviving the present. Now we started planning, nesting. Truth began to make amends for his lack of presence with his daughters. I talked with Tessa, the eldest, on the phone soon after we moved in to the house. She had just graduated from High School and we committed, as a couple, to pay for her college. I wanted stability, and a family. I knew this was the first step for him and necessary before we could even think about having our own children.

One night about a month later, as it poured with rain outside, Truth and I cooked in the kitchen. He never used recipes and just started throwing ingredients into the pot, and his creations always tasted great. As he chopped the vegetables and I mixed a salad he said out of the blue "If something ever happens to me, I want you to look out for my girls." Of course, I said. Sure. I changed the subject. He told me the same thing a month later in the den while we watched a movie. "Shut up Truth, don't talk like that."

Truth still worked seventy or more hours in the business. I pulled forty to fifty hours most weeks. I wanted the business to flourish and grow bigger. I wanted the financial benefits. I wanted to buy a house. I wanted kids. But I hated working the insanely long hours. Most of the time, I worked so hard only because I knew what would happen if I didn't. Often I sat at my desk pretending to be working and imagined a different life.

I put my head down on the glass desk and closed my eyes falling into fantasy. This time I drove down the highway in Los Angeles in a convertible my long red hair blowing in the wind. With no traffic, I flew down the road with nothing inhibiting me. I stopped at a light and stretched my head back looking at the crisp blue sky, hearing the waves of the Pacific and I smiled. Alone. And happy. I was completely satisfied. In my dream, I was an actress driving to an audition practicing my lines in the car. No porn sites, no Truth, no fear, no fights, I felt free and couldn't stop giggling.

I sighed, opening my eyes, looking at my reflection in my monitor, all two hundred and ten pounds of zero self-esteem woman. *Who the hell was I kidding?* When I looked at the future that lay before me all I saw was a black hole with me falling through it.

Twelve

The last fight occurred on a scorching hot Saturday in July 1999; the kind of day fair skinned girls like me stayed inside in Las Vegas. Not in the mood for working, I switched on the television in the den for some background noise while I vacuumed. The World Cup finals featured the women's USA soccer team playing China. I loved women's sports, and quickly became engaged in the match. I forgot about all the cleaning and instead plopped down, sinking into the plush tan sofa. A hundred thousand screaming fans packed the stands- all cheering the women to victory. The energy mesmerized me. Truth came down the stairs bounding into the kitchen.

"So is this what you're doing all day?"

"Shhhhhh. I'm watching this."

I heard him pouring himself a big glass of juice.

"I thought you were in your office."

"Just a minute… I'm watching this."

"When are you gonna be done?"

"A minute … give me a minute." I dreaded going upstairs and working. My main computer I used for marketing crashed the night before. Afterwards he spent hours reloading software; I promised him I would go back this afternoon and back up all my files. I didn't want to be doing that kind of boring, monotonous work, not on such a fine summer Saturday.

The game went into overtime and still tied, 0-0. A Chinese girl kicked the ball, and at the last minute one of the American girls kicked it out foiling their winning goal. The game was about to go into the penalty round where one of these teams would win.

"Now, Amy."

"I said I'll go and I will, but in a minute. This is really good."

I heard him mumble, walk up the stairs and slam the door to his office. There hadn't been a tornado in months, so I wasn't in alarm-mode.

The commentator explained what would happen next, five kicks by the Americans and five by the Chinese. If still tied, they would do a kick off. The penalty kicks were taken from right in front of the goal; they only had to kick the ball twelve yards past the goalie into the net. The challenge was not kicking one in as much as for the goalie to stop the goal from being scored. The American goalie was a young Black woman named Briana Scurry. What pressure. Everything came down to these final moments. The Chinese won the coin toss, and they went out and scored their first point. The first American player, Carla, walked out to the field. She scored one point as well. The mostly American crowd roared.

I sat with legs crossed on the coffee table three feet in front of the TV bouncing up and down with the crowd. I turned the volume up to tune out Truth's bitching and moaning, which I could sense even from this distance. I turned the volume up too loud on purpose. I wanted to piss him off. *Yes I'm gonna sit here all day if I damn well please, watching TV, and yes I'm going to turn up the volume.* While most of my listening remained on the game, about twenty percent of me intently focused on what was happening upstairs. I heard his footsteps over the hardwood floors in his office. I heard him open and slam his door and walk heavy-footed into our bedroom.

The second Chinese woman scored and the second American woman also scored. It was 2-2. I cheered for Briana. You can do it, girl!

Chick chick. I knew that sound. It was the chick chick of the shotgun and his feet marching back down the hallway and then to the stairs and now coming down the steps.

"Is this where you want to take this?"

I turned from the game and saw him standing at the foot of the stairs, his eyes fuming with the shotgun pointed at the ceiling. *Oh shit. Not now.* The third Chinese woman stood in front of the ball.

"No," I said.

I turned back to the game. She missed it! Briana blocked the kick! The crowd went crazy; the screams from the TV filled the room. The American women were now winning. He walked over to where I sat and flipped the switch off. Silence.

"Is this where you want to take this?" he repeated as if I hadn't heard him the first time.

When he turned off the TV, something clicked inside of me. My mind went chick chick. I was sick and tired! Fed up with this same old scene being played out over and over between us. I looked straight at him with defiance and picked up the remote and turned on the TV.

I stood up and got right in his face. "Go ahead and get it over with ... shoot me." My face turned red from my anger. "Go ahead – do it! Just do it now. Get it over with!" I wanted to attack him.

Push him over, take the gun from him, but I didn't dare. I stood two inches from his face fanning the flame; enraged that he interrupted the most crucial part of the game.

His eyes turned pitch black, the pupils smaller than normal, his right nostril flared. His breathing was deep and heavy when he turned from me and began walking back and forth in the living room around where I stood. "Is this what you want?" he yelled looking away from me. The threats replaced most of the physical violence and the guns were enough to keep me in line so he didn't need to lay a finger on me. I wanted to see this game end. I didn't care if I won or lost at this point. I wanted it over.

"Do it then! What are you waiting for?" I taunted him. I felt reasonably sure he was bluffing. 97% sure he would not pull the trigger. I imagined myself attacking him, scratching his eyes out. You are disturbing my fucking game!

I turned back to the TV; the Chinese woman, fourth to kick, stood silent focused on the goal in front of her. The crowd howled.

He pumped the gun, chick chick and pressed it against my forehead. I closed my eyes and listened to the crowd roar. I was strangely calm. I felt nothing. I waited for the explosion.

Nothing.

Silence except for the screaming on the television.

Nothing.

I knew it wasn't going to come; I let out a guttural scream. He turned from me with a start. I switched off the TV and threw the remote at the glass sliding door that led to the patio. It shattered and two double A batteries flew out. I ran into the living room and guest bathroom, locking the door behind me. I stepped into the shower, which had never been used since we moved in; I closed the glass door behind me and curled up on the shiny white tile floor. I hugged my legs tightly to my chest, rocking back and forth. I rocked shaking my head. I couldn't cry or talk or think or feel anything. I just rocked. I wanted out, out, out! I wanted an end to my life, as I knew it. I considered turning on the cold water – I wanted to feel the coldness on my face, but I couldn't reach the faucet from where I sat, and I didn't feel like getting up. All I could do was rock, my eyes wide open, my sockets stretched beyond their normal capacity. The bathroom, my sanctuary, the small space, white walls, coldness of the tile all comforted me. It had been the place of my retreats for the last four years when it got too scary. I knew I was trapped. Stuck. I knew it was not going to end. All I could do was rock. Rocking was the summation of my being able to help myself. My unbridled, fast rocking slowed down to a medium-paced, soothing rocking and down to a barely moving rocking. Then I stopped.

I crawled out of the shower, oblivious to where Truth had gone in the house. The bathroom door remained locked, and since he had never broken the door down, I felt safe. I stood up at the sink and looked at my face – my pale skin was the color of a tomato. I ran my fingers under the cold water and splashed my cheeks. I began to see some of the redness retreat. I felt no connection to the reflection in the mirror, to the blob of flushed skin and round nose and green faraway eyes with bushy eyebrows and thick bottom lip with teeth indentations faintly present. Why can't you just leave? What is wrong with you? Leave. Just go. Only ten short yards separated the bathroom from the entryway of the house. Open the door and run for your life.

"I can't." A voice came from inside. "I can't leave him. I don't know why."

Whatever. My faraway eyes looked on with disgust at my reflection in the mirror. Whatever. I heard a knock at the bathroom door.

"Are you ok?" I heard Truth's voice, soft now. Coming to make up—the honeymoon stage again so soon.

Somehow, without my knowledge, my life had turned into reruns, the same show running over and over with no hope for new episodes. I had been cancelled and didn't even realize it, didn't even bother to watch my own season finale. My beat up black and white TV only picked up one station – my shitty, mediocre life.

I unlocked the door and let him in; his eyes looked calmer, a lighter caramel shade of brown, watery like he had been crying. Things will be different next time. I'm really trying. He put his arms around me, and I stood limp in his embrace. Yes, I must have said. I walked over and flipped on the TV. The game had ended, and I missed who won.

Thirteen

The only thing about tragedy that makes it tolerable is the deep feeling you have that there is not a damn thing you can do. The gods have intervened. In retrospect I see throughout most of my relationship with Truth, I (and I think I can say we) were unplugged from the universe. Disconnected. Unconscious. If you said this to me at the time, I would have laughed in your face. *Unplugged my ass. Whatever I would say … fucking kooky new age people.* On September 28th, 1999 we got plugged in, but not of our own free will.

We went to the grocery store that Sunday evening and rented some movies. We watched *The Matrix* in the living room while dining on breakfast food – omelets, toast, and sausage. I left the movie early to take a bath. Truth finished watching and came upstairs to the bedroom. Our sex life had become a once a week affair; one which I didn't often look forward to. However tonight I felt amorous. I got dressed up for him, something at this point in our marriage I rarely did. I wore a white baby doll negligee and thigh high white stockings. He looked at me as I came out of the bathroom. Even with my rotund body he said, "God you're beautiful," like he had forgotten and rediscovered me. We didn't make it to the bed, making love on the rose colored carpet. Our energy together felt different, intimate and new.

I dressed noticing the carpet burns under each knee. We returned to our offices to get some late night work done. Just after three A.M., Truth came running out of his office clutching his chest.

Truth went into the bedroom and lay down. I followed asking questions.

"What's going on?" My head began to spin as it always did during crises, and I was having a hard time being present.

"I don't know," he said, a little angry.

"What can I do?"

Truth had a history of high blood pressure and he took medication for it. He also had a mild case of pneumonia the previous Christmas. Otherwise, he had never been sick.

"My stomach hurts. Something doesn't feel right."

"We should call a doctor." I was always quick to call for help.

He looked up at me scared. Truth hated hospitals. Fifteen minutes later, I picked up the phone and he ran over, grabbing it out of my hand.

"I don't need a doc ..." he didn't even get the whole sentence out before he started to vomit and ran into the bathroom. Dread, panic, and rage ran though my veins all at once.

"I am trying to help you!" I yelled into the bathroom but I could only hear moans and more vomiting.

"I'll be ..." more vomiting "fine. I must have just eaten some bad food."

Some bad food. Ok, maybe that was it. And once I implanted this thought into my head I almost forgot about the chest pains.

I knew better than to call 911 if he didn't want me to. I tried to comfort Truth and keep him calm. He had excruciating stomach pains. It was like the most dreadful hell of a soup we were cooking. Truth's terror grew by the second, as I'm quite sure he knew the seriousness. His fear increased the anger he was expressing towards me, which then increased my fear and anger and rage, and the pot was about to explode. After vomiting up everything in his stomach, he collapsed into the bed. We had no idea what was wrong. An hour later he realized he could not move his right leg. We still thought food poisoning but inside both of us knew food poisoning wouldn't do this. I rubbed his leg for him and we soaked it in warm water.

He gave in and told me to make the call. I had never called 911 before. I had thought about calling many times, threatened to call a few times but never actually did. A woman answered; professional and calm, she asked some questions about symptoms and said they were sending someone over. The paramedics arrived about twenty minutes later just as dawn broke on a Monday morning still on the tail end of a furiously hot summer. I ran downstairs to let in the two men carrying medical cases and a stretcher. They walked upstairs to where Truth lay in our bed. At this point he could not walk, his right leg completely numb.

The first EMT guy took Truth's blood pressure. The expression on his face when he read the numbers is seared into my memory. While I was in, "everything is going to be fine now that help is here," overdrive mode, if I had been seeing clearly, I would have known what his look meant. People with blood pressure this high don't live long. I quickly turned my mind to other things. Truth would need a change of clothes and perhaps some books to keep him occupied in the hospital. I imagined he'd be sitting around looking for things to read. So I grabbed the latest edition of "Computer Shopper," from his office along with my purse while the two men carried him downstairs on the stretcher, sliding him into the ambulance. I took the Camry and raced behind them. I remained highly optimistic all this would be figured out, and I'd need the car to drive him back home.

Fourteen

I always believed in the power of authority figures, or should I say that I've always *given* them my power, the way I gave Truth my power? I liked it that way. I wanted to live in a world that you can trust everyone. Medical doctors spend many years in school, and have a calling to save lives. I made all these assumptions. I believed that once we got to the hospital everything would be fine.

Early on a Monday morning we found ourselves in a packed emergency room, but luckily a patient with blood pressure as high as Truth's got a little priority. Not that it did a lot of good. The doctors and nurses were sure of one thing – he was very sick. They just didn't know why. In fact, they had no idea. I sat by his side in the ER watching the doctors come in and poke and prod. He said little but let out moans, and I knew he had excruciating pain in his leg. They gave him medication to bring his blood pressure down and pumped him full of morphine. The ER doctor assigned his case to a primary care physician, and we waited five hours in the ER for a room to open up on the ICU.

I walked by his side as they wheeled him into room 224, the first room on the right side just as you walked in the double doors from the hallway and waiting areas, directly across from the nurse's station. We had no idea who his doctor would be. We had a new HMO that we signed up for when we moved to Vegas, and since Truth had not seen a doctor yet, they picked one for him; a bit like rolling dice but we had no choice.

Dr. Tomás was a woman from some Eastern European country of which I am unfamiliar – one of those countries that used to be called something else. I didn't have any choice but to trust her, so I didn't fight it. I could tell upon first meeting her that she cared for her patients, and I felt a maternal feeling coming from her. And I could have used my mother right now. It never occurred to me not to trust her.

"Your husband is very sick. I am ordering many tests and will do my best to discover what is wrong." That's what she told me in her thick accent after examining him for the first time and reading through the intake chart. Dr. Tomás had Truth in and out of tests all afternoon and into the evening. She ordered chest and abdomen x-rays, ultrasound of the pancreas and gallbladder, and arterial ultrasound of the lower extremities.

Even with these test results, she didn't understand what was wrong with Truth. And even more unfortunate, since we had an HMO, and HMO's hate paying for expensive angiograms and specialists, not a whole lot was done for the first day and a half in the ICU. 36 hours feels like a lifetime when you're watching your husband deteriorate in front of your eyes. I watched the fear and dread take over his face. I tried to smile and stay upbeat and not show my terror. I tried to smile and not show my confusion about this man I both loved and feared. For the first time *I was in charge of him*, of his health, of his being, and it scared the living daylights out of me.

Looking back, I don't know how I got through those hours. Most people have no clue how much they can cope with. I flat out refused to believe this situation would end badly, and I trusted the doctors. Strangely, I felt safe. From the time Truth fell ill, I felt protected by forces I cannot explain. I felt plugged in, but to what I could not say.

I prayed a lot. I wasn't raised in a religious or spiritual family, and I didn't know much about praying. I was the pray-only-when-you're-in-an-emergency type of girl – the one who only thanked God after a near miss in traffic. I said a lot of *Please God* and a lot of *Oh God* the first day, not graceful at all. When not praying, I watched the numbers. There's not much else to do in the ICU but watch the numbers on the machines: Heart rate, oxygen level, and blood pressure. Each number had a different optimal level, which I quickly learned. As the numbers moved closer to the desired level, my insides relaxed. Then the number would move away from normal range even by just a point and I would tense up again.

Tense.
Relax.
Tense. Tense. Tense. Tense.
Relax. Relax.
Tense.
Relax.
Tense. Tense. Tense.

If I had been a wiser girl, I would have gone outside and gotten a cup of coffee and breathed the fresh air. If I had been a wiser girl, I would not have lost touch with every last friend, and I would have called one up to come stay with me. If I had been a wiser girl, I wouldn't be here. I wouldn't have let him punch me or threaten me with bullets and words. I would have left and not returned. If I had been a stronger, wiser girl, I would be leading some support group tonight for former battered wives. I would be counseling other women on how to save themselves. But I wasn't so wise or so strong. And there I sat watching over this man I loved.

By nightfall on Monday, I stopped watching the numbers because I couldn't bear it. I became a pacer. I paced the loop of the ICU around the nurse's station like an Indy 500 driver. Each time I came around I would look in on Truth, take a quick glance at the numbers, give him a big loving smile and blow a kiss and then back out on the track. I no longer trusted the doctors. I raced right up to the nurses' station and asked for a phone book. I had this insane notion I would just go to the "P" section and start calling physicians, and get one to drive over here and tell me what was wrong. At ten o'clock at night. "I have money," I would say. "I'll pay you whatever you want."

Both of his feet were stone cold. The nurses could not find a pulse in his right leg – not even with a highly sensitive machine called a Doppler device.

Dr. Tomás put an order in Truth's chart to page her if the arterial ultrasound turned up something. No one paged her. I didn't know this at the time. I only knew he was deteriorating quickly and no one was doing anything. I fumed furious and terrified but tried to keep it all from Truth. I tried my hardest to be a pillar of strength and calm for him – *everything is going to be okay.*

I marched up to the nurse's station for the fifth or sixth time complaining something should be done. I screamed at them like Shirley McClain did when her daughter lay dying in *Terms of Endearment.*

"He needs a doctor – he needs someone that can diagnose what the hell is wrong. He needs one now. Right now!" I surprised myself with the force of my words. That's how Pat would talk. I stood refusing to move until all the nurses snapped out of their work daze and acknowledged me freaking out under their fluorescent lights.

"One of you needs to do something. Now!"

About an hour later they sent in the on-call doctor – another doctor from another country I did not know the name of: Dr. Kirav, a dark haired man in his late thirties. He walked into Truth's room and examined him for about two minutes; he felt his legs.

"With ten as the worst pain you've ever experienced and zero as no pain, how are you feeling right now?"

Truth could talk but was very weak and groggy from the morphine.

"Nine"

"Where does it hurt the most?"

"Leg, foot, stomach."

Dr. Kirav jotted notes in the chart. I stood a few feet away from the bed observing every move he made, and I pulled a small wire bound notebook from my purse and started taking my own notes of all the activity.

He began to walk out and I stopped him "What are you going to do?" It seemed like a pretty good question to me.

"Your husband is very sick. He'll get a thorough examination in the morning when his primary care doctor comes in. In the meantime, I'm upping his pain meds."

I can't believe I accepted his answer. I wanted to jump on his back and tackle him to the ground. DO SOMETHING! I wanted to scream. Don't tell me he is sick, I know that – do something to make him better!

I said none of this. If something needed to be done, he would do it – a voice inside said argued with me. He is a doctor after all. I stood in the doorway and watched Dr. Kirav inside the nurse's station writing his notes in Truth's file. I scrutinized and listened as he flirted with the nurse on duty, a young, attractive brunette.

"No … I'm not the expert here … imagine you are …" I heard him say to her. She giggled. The 'don't rock the boat', good girl voice in side of me choked at this point, and I realized I was completely on my own. This was not a safe place. I made the wrong assumptions. I jotted down everything in my notebook, and contemplated how I could get my very sick husband out of this hospital.

I knew the first thing we were going to do once Truth got out was to see an attorney. I turned and walked back to hold Truth's hand.

"Everything's going to be okay. I love you Baby. I love you and everything is going to be okay."

I kept saying the words over and over like a mantra – to him, to me, to anyone in the universe who would listen. And despite the seriousness, despite this enormous mess we found ourselves in, I somehow knew that we would survive. At the time, I could not explain the feeling my senses picked up. I could not explain them because I had never been open to them before. What I believe I felt was God. In the midst of all the terror, I felt protected. We were both protected. How strange.

On Tuesday morning, Truth still did not have a diagnosis. At midday, a pulmonary specialist named Dr. Andrews made his rounds in the unit when he overheard me complaining to the nurses. He walked in and took a look at Truth. At 12:15 pm, Dr. Andrews examined him for five minutes. By 12:22 pm he had signed off on three orders to a nurse and scheduled an emergency angiogram to confirm his diagnosis of acute terminal aortic occlusion with thrombus. In layman's terms he told me, Truth, in all likelihood, had a blood clot, and it had blocked off the blood flow to his legs. He put three doctors on call for an emergency aorto-bifemoral bypass once he confirmed the diagnosis. He proclaimed out loud, "this patient is within hours of complete respiratory failure." I almost jumped on him and covered his mouth – "sshhhh not in front of him," I wanted to say. I knew it was his body, and he probably already knew, but I still wanted to protect him. Despite Dr. Andrews' lack of bedside manner, I was relieved someone knew what was going on here. Finally the cavalry had arrived.

The angiogram results showed exactly what Dr. Andrews suspected. A top vascular surgeon was brought in to perform the surgery. Dr. Moore looked like a runner with his tall, intelligent, slender 40-something body. I knew the runner's look a mile away, and I never met one I didn't like. I imagined him running five miles every morning as the desert sun rose before coming to the hospital to operate on men's hearts. Men like Truth, and his heart.

His heart. My stomach sank inwards. Shit. His heart.

I couldn't sit still so I kept moving, pacing. If I stopped moving then the weight would catch up to me; but if I stayed one step ahead, I could beat it.

Dr. Moore sat down with me in the waiting room and drew a sketch showing me what he would be doing to Truth in the surgery. He didn't sugar coat the situation: "We'll do our very best to make sure he makes it off the table. His chances are about fifty-fifty."

Just like the odds of betting black on a roulette table. "Always bet on black," Truth would say with a wink and a smile. I never played Roulette, and I had no idea how this game would end.

Dr. Moore rushed off to suit up for the surgery. For the first time, I noticed the round moist stains of sweat under my armpits. I still wore the clothes I had put on hastily when the ambulance arrived – black pants with elastic waist, a faded navy blue t-shirt and my favorite old pair of running shoes. I had not brought any other clothes to change into, and I had no one to call to bring them to me. I had not washed or brushed my teeth since Sunday night. I became aware I didn't look or smell so wonderful, but it was the least of my concerns.

I closed my eyes tapping my right foot rhythmically. I focused my attention on the movement. It was a large waiting room with four different sofas, about a dozen chairs with tables in each corner loaded up with magazines. Two other people shared the room with me: one teenage boy stretched out sleeping across four chairs completely oblivious to my presence and a middle age white woman in the corner watching TV. I wondered how long the boy had been here and why he was stretched out asleep on the chairs rather than on the sofa. The sofa seemed like it would be more comfortable. I wished I could be in his world, in his life, to relax enough to fall asleep.

My foot still tapping, I began to quietly cry. I had always been able to hold back tears, but the stress of the last thirty-six hours had worn down my defenses. So many different emotions ran through my body that they had to stand in line. Terror and fear were at the front, but behind them at least ten other less powerful emotions stood waiting their turn. They couldn't quite compete with terror and fear, but they still made their presence known. It's excruciatingly uncomfortable to experience sharply conflicting emotional states at the same time inside your mind. It's enough to make you feel like you're going crazy.

The thoughts chased each other. *Please God, I love him so much. Please make him better. I can't lose him.* This thought led the pack, but closely followed by: *This is what you get! This is what you and your wife-beating ass gets!* My emotions had been thrown into a giant gladiator's ring to fight it out. I knew only one would make it out alive. *I love him. I am so worried and afraid* came out with no weapons and lay down in the center of the ring. *I hate you for what you put me through* came charging out spike in hand. *It's my fault this happened. I should have been a better wife* ran behind him pleading with him to be calm and put the weapon down. Next, *Don't worry everything will be just fine* came out and started hugging everyone else and finally, *Come on guys … It's not really that serious* walked out and tried to convince the others to go get some food. My head raged and I felt like I would pass out from the gladiatorial goings on inside.

When I came back to reality, the teenage boy still slept on the chairs, and the middle-aged woman still stared robotically at the TV, playing the same twenty-four hour news program.

A memory popped into my awareness of my high school Latin teacher, Mr. Greco, known for his military like discipline. I liked the control he maintained as it meant less idle time for my shy repressed high school self to suffer through. I liked not suffering. Also, he was a serious runner, so I had a deep respect for him. I remembered some advice he gave us once. He explained how to act if ever captured as prisoners of war. He was that kind of guy, giving helpful tidbits of information to his students like what to do in the event you become a POW. His tip involved chanting the Lord's Prayer in Latin over and over to kill time. The repetitious nature of chanting would keep our mind off the fact that we were POWs. We recited it every day for four years before class started, so I knew it well. Why not? I thought.

I paced back and forth in the waiting room reciting: *Pater Noster, qui est in caelis, sanctificatur nomen tuum, adveniit regnum tuum, fiat volentus tua, sicut in caelo et terra* nostra. It's amazing how easily it came back to me even though I hadn't given it a second thought for over nine years.

The woman, with freshly set hair, looked over at me. My Latin chanting must have distracted her from CNN.

"Are you here all alone?" she asked.

"Yeah. My husband's having surgery … emergency surgery on his heart."

"Where's your family?"

"We don't have any family here. We just moved."

"I'm sure he's going to be okay. This is a good hospital. My daughter's having knee surgery."

I stopped crying and we both stared at CNN for a minute.

"What were you saying before?"

"The Lord's Prayer. I only remember parts in English but I know the whole thing in Latin."

I smiled shyly because it sounded ridiculous.

"Do you want to sit over here by me?"

I walked over and sat in the chair next to hers. I let her take my hand.

"Do you want to pray together?"

I nodded my head.

Our Father, who art in heaven, Hallowed be thy Name. Thy kingdom come. Thy will be done, on earth as it is in heaven. *Pater noster, qui es in caelis, sanctificetur nomen tuum.* Adveniat regnum tuum. *Fiat voluntas tua, sicut in caelo et in terra.* Give us this day our daily bread. And forgive us our trespasses, As we forgive those who trespass against us. And lead us not into temptation but deliver us from evil. *Panem nostrum quotidianum da nobis hodie, et dimitte nobis debita nostra, sicut et nos dimittimus debitoribus nostris. Et ne nos inducus in temptationem, sed libera nos a malo.* For thine is the kingdom, and the power, and the glory, for ever and ever. Amen. *Quoniam tibi est regnum et potestas et gloria in saecula. Amen.*

We prayed together in English and Latin with CNN in the background while the teenage boy slept. Every few minutes the elevators would open with a ding and someone in green or blue or burgundy scrubs would walk out and down the hall to the ICU. About twenty minutes later her daughter got out of her surgery, and she left to be with her in the recovery room.

"Please take care of yourself."

I said goodbye and remained sitting. I decided to alternate Latin and English. I hoped God appreciated my multi-lingual prayer for help.

At 10:30 pm, roughly five hours after the surgery had begun, Dr. Moore walked out of a door on the other side of the waiting room from the ICU. I could tell by his face Truth was still alive, and a wave of relief washed over my body. He sat next to me and explained when they opened up Truth they expected to find an occluded artery. They did find a completely blocked artery and as a result it stopped the blood from flowing to the right side of Truth's body. They fixed the occlusion by replacing with a graft part of the artery in the lower abdomen and where it descends into the femoral artery. They didn't expect to find the original cause of the blockage was a split, a dissection of his aorta. Truth's aorta where it entered his heart had split into two. The technical term is Aortic Dissection and it's not uncommon in men in their seventies and eighties but is almost unheard of in men in their thirties. The split caused the aorta to separate into two smaller tubes instead of one large one. The second tube terminated just below the heart and that saved Truth from dying instantly as it kept the dissection from going any further. Truth would need a second surgery to fix the dissection. They could not do the second procedure at the same time. The hospital didn't even have the machine needed to do the second open-heart surgery. Once he recovered he would have to be taken by Medevac to another hospital for that surgery. My hope of us returning to work in a few days had long since passed. I couldn't even comprehend the prospect of a second five-hour heart surgery.

Dr. Moore gave me the straight facts about his recovery chances. The first 24 hours would be touch and go. He might not survive the night. If he did survive, then he'd have a slightly better chance of surviving the next 24 hours and then the next, and the next. We would take it one hour at time. He told me about the risks of infection after surgery and that he'd be kept unconscious and on a respirator for three to seven days while his body healed enough to breathe on its own. I listened, but all I could think about, the only thing I cared about – he had made it. Always bet on black.

Fifteen

I had called my parents Monday afternoon about 6 P.M. interrupting their vacation with my mom's family in England. My dad could tell by my voice I needed him. He could always tell; I didn't even have to ask him to come. Now just over thirty hours later, and after a long flight from London to New Orleans and then onto Las Vegas, he stood next to me ready to help. Mom flew back with him but stayed in New Orleans to work. She wasn't good in emergencies. Dad would stay as long as needed.

Seeing Dad's burley white hand holding the deep brown fingers of Truth made me extremely proud of him and how far he'd come. He changed so much since Truth came into our lives. I hadn't told anyone about my abusive marriage. Partly because I felt ashamed, but also afraid if I did, my dad would go back to his old ways – back to being prejudiced.

Truth had become the 'go to' person whenever my family had computer problems. He impressed my dad with his intelligence. He'd charm my mother too, pushing her to learn for herself.

"Truth, dear, my printer is acting up again. I tell it to print and it takes about twenty minutes before it actually starts printing," my mom lamented on one of her weekly visits.

"I won't fix it. I will, however, teach you how to troubleshoot it so you'll be able to do it on our own next time" Truth replied.

"But I don't know anything about these things."

"Of course you do" Truth said laughing.

Mom looked at him politely smiling but insisted she really could not fix her computer problems "No, I really don't know."

"Of course you do." The way he said it, "OF COURSE you do," said with such impeccable conviction that for a second mom's eyes got wide and she opened up to him, as though maybe she did know. Maybe he knew something about her that she did not even know. He had a way of making you question deep-set beliefs that appeared to be closed books.

"You can learn. It's really not hard at all." And he sat with my Mom and went through the steps of resolving her printing problem, making sure she took notes.

"Next time this happens, I bet you can repair it without me."

Both of my parents had grown to love Truth. And Dad grew to respect Truth – as a man and as his equal. I never wanted to mess it up. I never wanted to give my parents any reason to disrespect him. So my father came to the hospital not just for me but also for Truth. Truth needed him, and I needed him.

The rest of the family began to trickle in. Truth's only sibling, Barbara flew in from Oakland. She had been through her own share of heartbreak from men, and she had come out a rock solid, confident woman who took care of herself. She lived with her German boyfriend, and they ran a lucrative supplements company together. Barbara had a successful career as a professional bodybuilder; at her peak she ranked as one of the top five in the world. I observed Barbara handling the string of doctors and nurses now caring for Truth. She stayed with her mother through cancer and knew how to deal with the hospital system. I watched and learned. Aggressive and proactive, she refused to allow the doctors to leave before we understood everything they said and had all our questions answered. She didn't let her emotions rule her.

The lack of medical attention in the first thirty-six hours was more than being made up for. Truth now had a string of five different specialists who came in every day to see him: the vascular surgeon who saved his life, the pulmonary doctor who first diagnosed him, a cardiologist, a renal specialist, a neurosurgeon in addition to his primary care doctor and a constant array of nurses, respiratory aids, and therapists. I even had a hospital counselor to guide me through the process of long-term ICU care. He had survived the first twenty-four hours, but they warned us to prepare for a long stay.

I spent most of my days and nights in a vinyl easy chair with legs propped up on a matching chair I had moved in from the next room. I took notes of everything and watched over Truth. I had nowhere else to go. I drove home for a quick shower once a day and rushed right back to the hospital.

It had been three days since Truth's aorta split at home; our business needed attending to, but I could do nothing. Truth handled all of the nightly programming jobs. Even if I did know how to run them, I didn't have the passwords to login to the servers. And Truth, still unconscious, couldn't give them to me. I accepted the fact that they would run automatically for a few days then the server logs would get full, and they would stop. Websites would go down. Customers would call and complain. Money would be lost. I could make some calls; find a company to hire to do the upkeep. I considered this as an option, but decided to wait. Five hundred men not being able to get their fill of naked women did not concern me. Losing money didn't bother me in the least. What did stress me was what Truth would do when he came out of this and discovered I let the business fall apart. I took a deep breath and let it go. I had more important concerns to deal with.

On day four, Dr. Sachs, renal specialist, informed me Truth's kidneys were not recovering as they should. I took another deep breath, "What does this mean for his recovery?"

"It's called Acute Renal Failure and is a complication we expected," Dr. Sachs said. "If his kidneys don't respond within twenty-four hours, we'll begin daily dialysis. The procedure puts a lot of strain on the heart, and we don't do it unless absolutely necessary but he's young so we can be aggressive." Yes, he's young. Young and strong.

Later in a medical library, I learned when the occlusion blocked the blood flow from one side of his body, it caused the muscles to go into a state of necrosis. The muscles released large amounts of various toxins, which can overwhelm the kidneys. By day five, his kidneys completely shut down. In the morning, an aid wheeled in the dialysis machine. As I watched it suck out all of Truth's blood, clean it and push it back into his veins, I dubbed it the Vampire machine. Now Truth would live forever.

My sister, Julie arrived and she, my dad and Barbara were my support system. I did not want Truth ever left alone. We broke up the day each one of us taking shifts. When I had time off, I couldn't sleep, not yet. Instead, I roamed the hospital. I walked up to the maternity ward and looked at the babies. The tiny adorable faces would greet me with their light and energy. I wondered what our babies might look like. Interracial kids always came out stunning; the joining of races must please God and so he rewards the babies with beauty. After visiting the newborns, I walked down to the chapel and sat tensely trying to pray. My body in a state of shock and overdrive made relaxation impossible.

I sat in the chapel on my knees, and I remembered as a child I used to be amazed at the durability of the human body. I thought about how much abuse our bodies can take. Like car crashes and stabbings and burns and gunshots and the body just takes it and heals itself. I thought the body could survive almost anything.

I meditated on the idea now watching Truth hooked up to the dialysis machine. Witnessing every ounce of his blood taken out of his body, recycled through and put back inside of him. Cherie operated the machine. She loved to talk, and I sat and listened, holding Truth's hand as she worked. Cherie said she was just doing this part time because the money wasn't bad, but she had much bigger dreams. She wanted to become a voiceover artist, like the voices in the commercials. She explained people always told her how smooth and sultry her voice sounded. She had a friend who knew a Producer in Hollywood, and once she got a demo tape made, she planned to give him a call. I nodded and smiled, trying to be sincerely excited for her new career plans. In my mind, if I befriended the nurses and therapists, the ones who pushed the buttons and inserted the needles, they would go the extra inch that might make the difference, as though Cherie had the power to heal him with some special incantation she could recite with her sultry voice, while operating the vampire machine. I wanted her to be in a good mood while she pulled his blood out of him. I didn't want to give her a reason to make any errors. I used whatever small amount of control I thought I had.

I talked to Truth a lot. I touched his hands. I stroked his skin. I looked at his closed eyes, and I watched the numbers on the machines. I communicated with him with my mind. I visualized my body's strength like millions of particles of light, and I used my power to send them over to his motionless body on the bed. I massaged his right leg, which he had not moved since being admitted. I would leave the medicine to the doctors and become a miracle worker. By sheer force of will and passion, I would heal his leg. I massaged it four times a day for twenty minutes at a time. I imagined my strong, healthy energy moving via osmosis into his skin and down to his muscles and cells. I would give life back to his leg. By midnight on the sixth night, after I finished his fifth massage, I sat next to him staring intently wishing, hoping, loving and projecting.

For the first time since he had been brought in, he moved his right leg. I wondered if I made it up, if I was seeing things. I ran out to the nurse's station and told the on call doctor to come in and look. The doctor witnessed him moving it again. Not a lot, but some movement there. I felt triumphant. Ecstatic! If I could heal his leg, I could heal his heart. I was an optimistic and driven girl. I could heal his heart!

They say hindsight is 20:20 and looking back I can say that I should have seen all this coming. I had chosen to fill my life with so much chaos, I could not see anything clearly. When I closed my eyes and thought of the future, I never imagined him unconscious in a hospital bed fighting for his life. My fear had been the police would arrest Truth. My worst fear was the police would shoot him. He would lose his temper somewhere in public and all hell would break loose

Early on the seventh morning, all hell did break loose. I had gone down to the cafeteria for tea and toast. Still feeling giddy with the idea that I could create miracles. Dad sat in the room when Truth woke up from the drug induced unconscious state he had been in for the past 5 days. He didn't know where he was, and awoke terrified. He pulled the tube which sustained his life out of his throat. His body wasn't ready to breathe on its own, and the machines screamed out with loud alarms. As I walked back into the ICU, I saw two nurses and a doctor rushing into his room. My heart began to surge as it did every time I saw a nurse or doctor running. They kicked Dad out as they started to work on him. We stood in the hallway listening and trying to see as it took four of them to physically restrain Truth and force the tube back down his throat. There was no end to the up and down ICU drama.

He was awake! Conscious. He could see me and touch me and hear me. After the doctors got the situation under control, I walked in and sat at his bedside. I took his hand in mine. He looked up with some effort and gave me a tiny smile.

"I'm so happy you're awake. Everything is going to be fine, baby. Everything is going to be just fine." I gave him my warmest, softest, strongest self. "I love you." And I did love him. Despite his rage, despite my rage at him for his rage, when I sat there with him love poured out of every cell in my body.

When he extubated himself, he ripped the vocal chord muscles so he couldn't talk. But that was the least of our worries. His kidneys had not responded to the dialysis.

Dr. Sachs brought me out into the hallway. The levels of CPK (creatine phosphokinase) in Truth's bloodstream was up to 47,000. Dr. Sachs said he had never seen levels as high. This was a measurement of an enzyme in the blood stream that is released when there is muscle damage.

"It might take two weeks of dialysis, a month or even two months before his kidneys respond. They might never respond. In this case since he's young, a transplant would be an option."

I focused my eyes on Dr. Sachs' glasses. "Okay." Not like an all right or good or no problem kind of okay but a I can't take any more bad news and can't do a damn thing about it kind of okay.

"We're treating your husband aggressively with the dialysis. Sometimes the kidneys simply need a jump-starting."

I don't think he actually said jump-starting, but I remember the image in my head of connecting jumper cables to Truth's kidneys. I had faith that his kidneys would come back to life. Besides, I couldn't deal with talk of future transplants, so I let that word float out in the distance- second open-heart surgery, possible kidney transplant.

On the seventh day, they brought in a new specialist to the team, one dealing with infectious diseases. A common occurrence with ICU patients who have been on a respirator is a massive infection called sepsis. They didn't bother to tell me that many people in the hospital don't die from their initial medical issue but from sepsis. Essentially being in the hospital can make you sick – a nasty little side effect of the ICU.

I couldn't take any of these new developments in and process what they meant. I just let the words bounce the surface – acknowledged them and let them fly off me. Usually, information gave me power. Growing up I loved the library. I would do research, seek to understand the situation and figure out my options. I had some control – usually. I knew I had no control in here, and it pissed me off.

"Ok" I said. "Sepsis. Fine. You anticipated it. Good. He's getting the right antibiotics. Excellent. He might be immune to the antibiotics. Okay, well you have others right? Good then. Just do it. Make him better."

On the ninth day, Truth still couldn't talk or eat. He took food intravenously, and ever since he had awoken, he was only allowed to suck on tiny sponges of water that I dipped in ice for him. I could tell he had begun to get restless with this program. I considered his agitation a sign of his healing.

He strained to get sound out, trying to talk but we could not understand him. Barbara and I brought in a small chalkboard and we eagerly handed him the chalk. He scribbled out his first clumsy word, as all his muscles needed rehabilitation. We looked over at the board and over at him. I think I expected something a bit more profound then what appeared to be S O M C. What the hell does SOMC mean? An acronym? What did he want to tell us? Then I noticed a faint dot above the second leg of the "M". I think the M was actually an "n" and an "i" connected together. Sonic. SONIC? Truth put his hand up to his mouth and pointed out the window. We let out a sigh of relief and laughter. That was the Truth we knew. Get me the fuck out of here and get me something to eat.

I wasn't about to actually let him eat a Sonic burger, and so began our first fight in the hospital. Day ten and the doctors said no food until they knew for certain his throat had healed. There was a risk that a solid piece could go down the wrong pipe and cause an infection. Because of the swelling, it would be almost impossible to intubate him again. His impatience began to spiral out of control. He did not like being told he could not eat. Had he not been hooked up to so many tubes, he would have just gotten up and left. The fact that he couldn't walk was the only thing that kept him there. His anxiety walked dangerously close to that line which would soon lead into anger. No one saw it but me.

On Friday, a vocal therapist came in to give him a test. If he passed, the doctors would let him eat. He had to blow hard enough to move a paper device and make some funny sounds. He blew as intensely as he could, but he failed the test. The vocal therapist had promised me that she would come in on Saturday to test him again. She had off for the weekend, but she told me she liked Truth and said she'd stop in anyway. If he passed the test, then she had the power to give him the Ok to eat. Otherwise she would not be back until Monday. I told Truth about this on Saturday morning, and he couldn't wait for her visit. He went through morning dialysis excited, and physical therapy in anxious anticipation. We waited all day, but she didn't show up. Truth was now thoroughly pissed.

"You lied to me. She was never going to come. Why are you lying to me?" his angry voice barely over a whisper. "You better tell me the truth. When I get outta here … you better have the police to protect you because you're gonna need it when I'm through with you!"

If not so exhausted, I would have laughed. It was a comical scene, a man who couldn't function without machines, couldn't walk, and could barely talk – threatening his wife with whispers. I wished I had the strength to laugh. But he was threatening me. Again. Part of me actually got scared. Again. I turned to run out of the room and saw that Barbara had been standing in the doorway. She had witnessed the whole fight. I ran through the double doors down the hallway and into the bathroom and curled up in the metal stall, I started crying uncontrollably. The tears poured out, my chest heaving. I couldn't believe he was back to this shit. After all that has happened, he's back to his old ways. Nothing will ever change. What kind of fucking idiot am I to put up with this? The thought occurred to me that now was my time to escape. Just run. Run for your life.

I heard someone open up the door to the bathroom. Barbara opened up the stall and looked down at me. I felt embarrassed she had witnessed our scene. I had never wanted anyone to know what things were really like between us. No one knew about the violence. I had told no one. I felt ashamed that I had stayed. I wanted to be strong. I wanted to be together when in reality I was ill, as ill as Truth laying in the ICU. If anyone opened their eyes to look at me they would see it. They didn't have to witness the fights to understand. That's if they looked. But most people don't see clearly, and it is very easy to appear fine. They don't want to know. Most of us don't live in a village; we live in distinct, separate prisons.

She knelt down next to me and for a minute didn't say anything while I calmed down. She helped me up, looked straight at me and said clearly and confidently:

"Once he gets better, you should leave him."

I didn't know what to say. Barbara would never have tolerated her brother's behavior. Not for a second. *Once he gets better … you should leave him.*

I'll deal with it then.

Sixteen

On Sunday, Dr. Tomás informed us Truth's prognosis looked good. The main question would be the level of permanent damage, if any. He might not even need the second heart surgery; they would test to see if the dissection could be treated with medication. My support system began their departure back to their daily lives. Truth's Dad had come out for a short visit from Seattle and left. Barbara and Julie had flights out later in the evening and would return on the weekend. Dad was staying with me as long as I needed him. He had the night shift at Truth's bedside, and I drove out to the Sierra Casino not far from our house. I felt a small pang of guilt; maybe, I shouldn't be in a casino while Truth lay in the ICU, but I desperately needed the break. I needed to hear the sounds of money clinking, of people laughing and drinking, signs of regular life.

Monday morning Truth had his dialysis and physical therapy. For the first time since he had fallen ill twelve days prior, he stood on his feet. He needed two therapists holding him up on either side, but it was a big step. I would use my mind's powers to fix his kidneys just like I had done with his leg. I placed my hands above where his kidneys lay, and I visualized my strength going into his skin, through his vessels and into his organs. I stared at the bag of urine connected to the catheter in his body. I visualized the urine dripping into the bag. Drip, drip drip … drip damn you! I envisioned the yellow liquid forming in the bottom of the plastic pouch. I sat next to him feeling one hundred percent focused and driven. Nothing could stop me.

I never had a chance to meet Truth's mom. She had died of cancer at fifty, only two weeks after Truth and I got together. She had three sisters, Diana, Louise and Robin. While we lived in the Bay Area, we visited with his three crazy aunties on a regular basis. They expressed the outward affection and love that I craved. My mom and dad showed me tenderness but it was more reserved, a quiet love. I wanted loud, raucous love. His aunties along with Truth's Grandma had planned a Vegas Girls Only Vacation months ago. I picked them up from their hotel Monday night, and brought them over to the hospital.

Truth was awake when they arrived. We spent about an hour talking and laughing with him. His grandmother, known as Grandma Ellis, had cleaned houses all her life. She saved her money and owned multiple properties across the country. In her mid-eighties, she still cleaned one house a week, just to keep her girlish figure. We talked about all the changes we'd make when he got discharged – a healthier, fuller, better life called us. We would take more time off and finally start a family. Truth looked tired, so I decided to take them back to their hotel and let him rest. Standing in the doorway to his room I mouthed the words "I love you". He mouthed them back with a smile, and I left.

Exhausted, I dropped his family off and drove back up north to our six-bedroom house that looked like every other six bed-room house on the block. I walked in the front door. Our cat, Squeak, ran up to my feet meowing vigorously. She wasn't used to being neglected. I sat down and watched as she gobbled up her food. I thought back to when we first adopted her after we moved in together and how cute our tiny orange kitten looked curled up in the arms of this beautiful man as he slept. I dropped my cell phone on the coffee table and stretched out on the sofa. I couldn't bear to sleep in our bed – even the thought made me sick.

I took a deep breath and exhaled trying to relax. I clenched and released each muscle group starting at my toes slowly moving up my body. The house was dark and silent except for the sound of Squeak nibbling up her salmon. I imagined what our relationship would be like when Truth came home. He is going to come home. I finally believed it. Would he be the same? Would he still get violent? Or would this near death experience change him, soften him? I got up to my thighs and I tightened the muscles and released. Up to my butt, I flexed and let go. I felt safe alone in the house like I could finally breathe.

Our sex life over the course of our marriage had severely declined. I couldn't fake sexual intimacy. I had taken to self-pleasuring on a nightly basis. For the first time since Truth fell ill, I touched myself. Like the casino trip, I experienced some guilt. I should not enjoy myself when Truth was so ill. But today we had crossed over the hump. I could celebrate. I could relax. I could release. I did, and then the phone rang.

The conversation with my Dad consisted of only a few words. "Come now. Don't get into an accident." I didn't have to ask him to explain. I grabbed my keys from the table and ran to the car.

10:30 pm on a Monday night the streets were empty, and I arrived in less than six minutes to the hospital; I raced up to the fifth floor. Dad walked through the door to the waiting room as I exited the elevator.

"His heart" my Dad spoke, close to tears. "I was with him, holding his hand and then something happened … They're doing that thing - the cart."

The image loomed in my head from dozens of movies. Crash cart. Paddles. That gel stuff they put on your chest. The electricity. Body jerks. Again and again.

"How long have they been doing it? How long have they been in there? Please go find out, I can't …"

Dad went back inside trying to get some answers. My body bent at the waist like something was pressing in on my stomach; I could barely stand up. This was NOT happening. Denial marched out in full force controlling the show. He was getting better. He stood up today. He was getting better! This is NOT happening. Not Not NOT happening. I repeated it over and over again like a five-year old having a tantrum. This is not how this will end. I felt nauseous and dizzy. A man sat reading in the lobby, paying little attention to my growing hysteria. I was angry. What's wrong with him? I'm gonna puke. I prayed frantically, "Our father, Our Father, Our Father Father Father Father, Hallowed be, Kingdom … come, come come … Pater Noster … Our Father … Our Father, Our Father."

For the briefest second, maybe even a millimeter of a second, if it could even be counted as a piece of time, the thought crossed my mind - *maybe I'd be better off if Truth died.*

Maybe I would be better off.

Screeeeeeeeccccccchhhh. Guilt crushed that thought with one fist and my next thought was I want him to live. *I want him to live. I love him!*

All my thoughts stopped when Dad walked back through the double doors from the ICU.

I wondered later exactly what time Truth passed on? I wondered if when I was cumming, he was going?

They have a special room on the ICU for people like me, so you don't bother the other patients and visitors. Isolating the freshly widowed makes sense; I wouldn't want to be around me either at that moment in time. You wouldn't even know the room exists unless you need it. About a hundred square feet, a love seat sat on one side and two chairs on the other. There were two corner tables one holding a phone and on the other a small digital clock. The room had no magazines or TV as this wasn't a waiting room. It was a mourning room, a breakdown room, a scream out to heaven because clearly God didn't hear your prayers room. It was a break the news to the others room. It was a room for everything that everyone else didn't want to witness – a parents losing child room, a children loosing parents room and in my case, it was a widow's room.

I sat down onto the loveseat and tried to breathe. In and out. Innnn and Outttt. Innnn and Outttt. My head had a constant low level buzzing preventing me from holding a thought. Dad sat down next to me and held my hand tightly.

"Sweetheart" he whispered, "we need to make some calls."

Calls. Calls. Calls. The word calls starting buzzing along with the noise in my head.

"Do it for me. Please. I just wanna sit here."

He started by phoning Barbara. I had the awareness of him talking to her, but I don't remember hearing the words. He hung up the phone. Decisions needed to be made. A young nurse walked into the room shutting the door behind her. I had never seen her before. She sat down next to me and put her arm around me.

"You know honey, in my experience with these things, it's important for you to go in and see the body."

The hair on my arm stood up as I heard her say *the body*. He was no longer a *he*. He was now just *the body*.

I didn't know that was important. I didn't really want to see it. I had never seen a …

I couldn't even say the "d" word. I couldn't comprehend the "d" word. My husband's "d" body was not a concept my brain could handle right now. The idea fell so far outside the boundaries of what I had ever expected I'd be doing at age twenty-seven. If the nurse said I should go see his body, that's what I would do. I rested on the sofa for some time; I'm not sure how long. I had the intention of getting up to walk about twenty yards to his room. I couldn't get my synapses to fire off the order to my legs to stand up. I looked up at my Dad and he held out his hand. I stood up with his help and walked.

Seventeen

Transformation doesn't happen overnight. It takes decades to shed our childhood conditioning – the beliefs and thoughts that pieced together like not so colorful charms on a bracelet determine our destiny. But sometimes one moment pierces a hole so large in our consciousness, we can't continue living as we once did. Seeing my husband's dead body was that moment for me.

Religion meant very little to me growing up. I was raised Episcopalian. Like Catholic but without the confessional. I attended Sunday school for about a year as a young child. My parents felt obliged to send my sister and me off to church, not because they believed in any of it, but because it seemed proper. After about a year, I think they grew weary of pretending and announced church was no longer required. At fifteen when I could drive, I went back a few times on my own. I liked the church and its 1960s mid-century design. It felt peaceful to me. And, I liked the priest. He was cute, and at 15 older men did something for me. I would kneel in the pew enjoying the atmosphere and fantasize about the priest – romantic fantasies, not sexual ones.

Dad was an atheist although he would never use that word for it. My mother was more of an agnostic. We never talked about God in our family although we did say grace, always the same prayer. *"Come Lord Jesus be our guest, let these gifts to us be blessed.*

Amen." We must have said it a thousand times. We didn't have a backup grace, and we never free styled it. That was the only time we ever mentioned Jesus, and I think we only said it to please my father's mother. I got most of my views on religion, God and Jesus based on my fathers' negative tirades about his sister. She was a born again Christian. My father thought the whole thing utterly ridiculous at best and highly dangerous at worst.

We never spoke of death. We never spoke of souls. We certainly never spoke of eternity. I had a clear picture of death: darkness. Death was pitch-black darkness. The coffin lid closes, the lights go out, and it's over - forever. I remember staying awake for hours in my preteen years thinking about infinity. I would lay stiff like a corpse and imagine what death would be like. Pitch black darkness forever and ever and ever and ever and ever. The *and evers* would torture me. I couldn't stop obsessing night after night. I decided I would stop thinking of death. From that moment onward, I became terrified of death. The thought, the image, the mere mention of the word made me go numb.

I stood by the door of his room. I had no concept of time so I can't tell how long. Then my body decided to move, and I took one step and another and another and with my fourth step I found myself right next to Truth's body, which was slightly slumped to the left.

What I witnessed when I looked into his eyes was the beginning of my own personal revolution. If seeing was believing, then I couldn't believe what was before my eyes. My husband, whom I had never spent a day apart from in four and a half years, was no longer there. He was dead. Yes, I knew that. His body, which the nurse insisted I say goodbye to, was not him. I knew it instantly when I looked into his eyes. He was nowhere to be found. Who I knew him to be had disappeared. Gone. I couldn't believe what I saw and what I felt in every pore of my being. *He was not there, but his body was.* So to whom was I saying goodbye?

I realize all this may sound elementary to those who were raised to believe in what I was just embarking on. I had no idea. My belief system told me it was him but dead. But it wasn't him. Was I going crazy? I found my presence there pointless. He wasn't there. I knew it just as much as I knew he *had* been there a few hours ago. So I left.

I had packed a plastic bag with clothes for Truth to wear when he got out, his favorite pair of long shorts, a blue t-shirt and sandals. They had been quietly tucked in a cabinet waiting for his release. I retrieved the bag, and looped my purse around my wrist and Dad and I left the hospital for good. We shuffled out of the ICU and through the waiting room; it could have taken us ten minutes to get from the ICU down five stories through the lobby and out to the parking lot. We made our way through the main doors of the hospital and outside; I felt fall in the air. When we had arrived twelve days before, it was still summer. Now fall had arrived, the Las Vegas version of it, a slight crispness to the air. Still dark, a tiny hint of the sun rose from the east. Just a peeping of sunlight, enough to say I'm here, I'm coming out soon.

As we inched across the parking lot my father holding my hand, the buzzing in my head quieted. I realized the gladiator fight had ended. All my emotions had fought their bravest most ferocious battle. Guilt and fear and terror and horror and anger and rage and sadness lay dying on the floor of my personal coliseum. Various degrees of injury and blood spilled from each one; I experienced their pain but in a muted sort of way. What remained, what walked out with me, standing tall, completely unscathed and beaming, was an emotion I had not felt these past two weeks.

I had never felt this sensation. The rumbling inside came as a complete shock to me. It was a new emotion, if you could even call this an emotion. It had snuck in at the last minute and completely decimated the competition. What I felt was a massive surge of relief from the realization that I had my freedom.

There was not a word in the history of words or a metaphor in the history of metaphors to describe how good I felt. My body looked catatonic, shell-shocked and unable to walk without help, but what I really wanted was to run and skip and jump. The realization hit me in the parking lot halfway between the door and the car.

I could do whatever I wanted,
Go wherever I wanted,
Talk to whomever I wanted,
Wink, smile, cry or laugh or scream or run,
Wherever I wanted and with whomever I wanted.
Forever and ever and ever and ever.
No one was there to stop me.
I was free.

Guilt was the least injured of all the emotions and tried to stand up and say something, but freedom stepped right down onto it. I knew what I felt. And my God did it feel good! And it smelt good. Freedom smells like WD-40, that sweet-smelling, purified petroleum raining down from the heavens making everything that is stuck, unstuck in an unexpected, miraculous moment.

And when I say I had no clue, just as I had no clue that Truth would be gone from his body, I had no clue I would feel like this. But I let it overtake me. Even if I couldn't express it then, I knew something was happening to me. Life had just begun for me. His death had brought me back to life.

Eighteen

We drove back to our house. It would take a long time to stop saying *our*. My father and I dragged the mattress down from the guest bedroom and onto the floor in the living room. Exhausted, we drew all the curtains and lay down on the mattress. My father started to cry and I held him.

"What are we going to do?" he said. "What are we going to do?"

It was a question he had asked before in my bedroom the first night he met Truth, but this time its meaning was altogether different. I was aware of the irony even then, even in the midst of the exhaustion and chaos. I felt numb but calm and more capable at that moment of comforting him.

I spent the rest of the day lying on the sofa in the darkness. I spent the first few days there. I barely moved. I had chest pains. I figured if Truth had died, so would I. We had been so close, so connected in every way possible I didn't think I could live if he died. I thought it would be a natural occurrence for me to go as well, like a two-for-one special. I was in and out of sleep for three days on the sofa. My father stayed busy cleaning, picking up, cooking for me and leaving plates of scrambled eggs and canned fruit on the coffee table next to me, even though I wouldn't touch any of it.

On the fourth day, I arose at sunrise with an idea. I drove myself to the Social Security office in Las Vegas, arriving ten minutes before they opened. I wanted to change my last name to Truth's. Even though I used his last name during our marriage, I had not officially made the switch from my maiden name. Suddenly, it was exceedingly important to me. It was a lot easier for me to be Mrs. Lewis after he was gone.

I was the first in line. "Congratulations" the Social Security clerk told me, obviously thinking I had just gotten married. Never mind, I thought, I'm not going to go there. But I was proud to take his name.

Even before we left the hospital, I signed the papers to order an autopsy. He had been getting better and there were questions that I needed answered. The doctors were not giving me the information I needed. His body was autopsied and then flown back to Oakland. We visited the funeral home that the hospital recommended and looked at the caskets. It was like a department store of caskets. And like any department store there was the bottom of the line caskets and the crème de la crème of caskets. I was ill prepared for the decision and pressure I would feel there. I looked to the funeral director for help.

"Well what kind of casket do you think he would like?" he asked, motioning to the mid-range models.

"What would he like? What kind of casket would he *like*? What difference does it make? I think he'd *like* to not be dead at 37." My anger came back to life with quickness.

I don't remember if I actually said that or just thought it. My bets are on *just thought it.*

He made the base line model look really plain, a basic pine box, something you bury people in who don't have family paying for it. I mean, who would get caught dead in a thing like that?

The model I picked out was bronze and cost close to five grand, which was too much money to spend to bury a dead body that didn't even belong to anyone I knew. Was I crazy? That's how I looked at it. It wasn't him.

My sister and mom flew from New Orleans to Vegas, and we drove as a family to Oakland. It was our first family road trip since I was fifteen. During the drive, I laid in the back seat of the car, staring out into the sky in daydream paying very little attention to my family or the scenery. As I gazed into the blue, fall sky with its big puffy cumulus clouds, I fixated on the question: where had he gone?

I knew he had *gone* somewhere. And I wanted to know where. It was all I could think about. I knew intellectually about the separation between body and spirit. But I had never actually experienced it. I had never felt it so clearly. He was not in his body. So where was he?

In my opinion, the funeral and burial were a sham. He certainly was not there. It wasn't him in the coffin so what were we doing there? The hypocrisy bugged me, but I didn't say anything. When we arrived in Oakland I spent the first day making plans for the ceremony with Barbara, Truth's aunties and his cousin. The young ones (me, Barbara and Roger) wanted the closing song to be Prince's *Let's go Crazy*. I can't remember whose idea it was, but I was all for it: *Dearly beloved, we are gathered here today to get through this thing called life.*

Truth loved Prince, but someone, I don't remember who, nixed the idea. The older folks wouldn't get it, they said. So we settled on Bob Marley's *No Woman, No Cry*. Which was fine, another good song Truth loved. I never quite got the meaning.

Was it woman don't cry or was it if you don't have a woman you won't be crying? I later looked it up on Wikipedia and they mentioned that many people did confuse the meaning. But in fact, it did mean, "woman don't cry."

It didn't work. I did cry.

The autopsy and the flight had bloated his face so looking at him now only strengthened my view that I was saying goodbye to a stranger. Who was this man? It wasn't Truth. But I was a sport so I played along. Since our broke days, Truth never left the house without at least a hundred dollars in his wallet. He had one particular hundred dollar bill leftover from when we first started to make money that he kept folded up in a secret compartment in his wallet. I took it out and put it in the pocket of his shirt. It's probably still there.

After the ceremony at the church, everyone drove about twenty miles up to the cemetery where he would be buried next to his mother. Truth and I had been there a few times to put flowers on her grave. The headstones were spread out over rolling hills overlooking the freeway. It was actually quite beautiful if you had your back to the freeway and looked out over the hills. I saw a white van driving up to where we all stood. I watched as they opened up the back doors and removed Truth's casket. I was furious. There had been a mix up at the funeral home, and no hearses were available to drive the casket, and the van was all they had. Truth would not be happy about this. How dare they take his body by van – a white van. He turned away the white limo they once tried to send us. He would have wanted a nice shiny black hearse. How humiliating, driven to his burial in a white van.

I let it go. What the hell was I going to do about it? And what difference did it really make?

I went through the motions of saying goodbye to his body, watching the casket lowered into the earth and placing a mixed bouquet of flowers on top before they covered it with dirt. I took my cues from what I had seen people do in funeral scenes in the movies, but I had very mixed feelings about it all. I was a woman caught into between two conflicting states. It was a place I was used to being in. On the one hand, I had the very clear and powerful feeling that Truth's spirit was not gone and much of this mourning business seemed, well, weird. But I had no proof of that and worse, it made me look like a bit of a crazy woman. I didn't know what to think. So I began to read.

Nineteen

After the funeral, my sister and mom flew back to New Orleans and dad came back with me to Vegas to close up house. Dad drove me to Barnes and Noble to buy some widow books. I looked to books to guide me and comfort me: "A Guidebook for the Grieving", "When There is No Time for Goodbye", "Widow", "Companion through the Darkness."

I read about the stages of grief, and knew I was still in shock. They advised me not to make any big decisions during this time - like moving. I ignored that one. There was no way in hell I was staying in Vegas by myself, and my father had to get back to work. I decided I would move back to New Orleans to grieve. It seemed like the best place in the world for that. A city built for the grieving.

After the funeral, I had gone to San Francisco and removed our servers from the data hosting facility where they ran. I hired another company to host and administer the sites. Once the sites were secure, and the money was flowing in again, I could focus my energy on grieving.

Before I left Las Vegas, I took a trip to Los Angeles to see a well-known medium, John Edwards, speak. This was before his TV show and media blitz. It was the first trip I had taken by myself in four and a half years. Dad seemed a bit surprised when I told him I was going to Los Angeles by myself. But as always, he knew I would do what I wanted. It felt good to board a plane by myself, to fly up in the air knowing I had picked the destination, that I was in charge of my days, of my nights that I could have gone anywhere. Could have changed my mind and decided I'd rather go to Tahiti. I could have gone to Italy, or Seattle or anywhere. I smiled at the idea that wasn't even an idea. I smiled at my reality. I teetered in between the woman experiencing freedom and joy for what seemed like the first time and the widow that I thought I *should* be. I got off the plane and boarded a small bus that took me to the hotel. I had only been to Los Angles once before so even the Culver City Radisson seemed exciting. The driver of the bus smiled at me as I got off, and I smiled back.

I smiled back!

And the earth didn't shatter! The tornado didn't touch down. I didn't have to walk home alone! There were no fights, no long silences, no waiting for the ball to drop. I smiled back, and it felt good. I walked into the Radisson and listened to a man speak who was famous for talking to dead people. The idea that was still an idea to me – still so far off from a reality to me – was just beginning to make itself at home in my head. He speaks to dead people. So does that mean they aren't really dead?

I flew back after the seminar and spent the next week sorting out our finances. Still that *our* … still so hard to say *my*. Truth didn't have life insurance. I had just sent off for an information packet a month before he got sick. It hadn't seemed important given our age and health. We had a small savings account, and we had the business. I was extremely happy for our portable porn business. My plan was to do the bare minimum to upkeep them, to keep money coming in while I figured things out.

I was lucky that I did not have to report to an office. I did not have to deal with pretending to be together. I could become as unglued as I wanted. I could experience every ounce of every emotion held in my body. I could cry until my eyes swelled shut, I could scream until my dad came running. I could hit and punch and collapse and let the pain roll over me and sleep until it was all gone. I felt extremely blessed for having the luxury to grieve.

Before leaving Las Vegas, I had two final errands to accomplish. The first stop was to the coroner's house to pick up the autopsy report. I'm not sure why we actually went to his house to pick it up (probably because we needed it faster than by mail); it seemed a bit too personal like we were picking up a coffee table we bought on Craigslist. No, we were picking up the pieces of paper describing in detail what the insides of my husband's body looked like. I was in a musky cloud of shock and gloom pierced only occasionally by a surge of energy to accomplish these final chores, as my father drove me there in the Toyota Camry. It was a part of Las Vegas I was not familiar with, miles from the sparkly, sprawling new subdivisions that all looked the same. This was an older part of the city, not far from downtown, where the houses looked like they were built many years apart.

I had not liked Las Vegas before Truth died, and now I had even more of a reason to despise every bump on every road, every streetlamp, stop sign, every brick, piece of stucco and neon tubing in this god-forsaken wasteland of a town. I ran up to his one story ranch style house shaded by a giant tree. Not in the mood for small talk, I knocked. He answered handing me a manila envelope. I don't remember if I thanked him.

As Dad drove me to my next appointment where these papers would be needed, I flipped through the report. He listed the cause of death as aortic aneurysm – basically the tube leading into the heart had exploded – complicated by sepsis. But if the heart exploded the sepsis seemed hardly important. Who cares about the chipping paint on your house if it gets blown away by a tornado? I turned to the second page "There are multiple tattoos on the body including a variety of unidentifiable entities. Many of these incorporate animals, sun-like devises and unidentifiable type creatures." Maybe he didn't want to write in the report about the sailor girl with tits that had been covered up when his second wife, the French one, pitched a fit. Was the sailor girl one of the unidentifiable creatures? I liked her; I always thought I couldn't believe I'm with this man who has a tattoo like this. Or was with. And the sun-like devises were tribal art that he got on some island in the Pacific, didn't this guy know anything? He got those tats done the island way, with a tortoise shell and needle thing. Hurt like hell but I'll never forget it I remember him telling me the story.

I skipped down further … "the nose is not remarkable." Bull-shit. It was remarkable. The way it flared when he was angry, the way it smushed into mine when we kissed hard, the way we gave each other delicate Eskimo kisses. I kept reading but stopped when I got to the section that described what was under the skin. I let my mind, for three seconds, go to that image of his body on the cold metal table being cut open and then I quickly closed the papers returning them to the manila envelope and throwing it into the backseat my voice quivering slightly as I told my dad "I think we need to go left here."

We parked and dad came with me as I went into to meet the attorneys at Taylor and Taylor Law firm, in their shiny, white one story office building. A father and two sons ran the firm – a family business. I had contacted one other attorney who turned down the case. He told me that medical malpractice cases were notoriously difficult, and unless it was a clear-cut case of malpractice then it would be very hard and very costly to win. Don Taylor, the fifty-something, good-looking patriarch of Taylor and Taylor, was not so pessimistic.

I recreated for him the events of the first two days when they didn't know what was wrong yet no specialist was sent in. I told him about the guy who came in that first night and then started flirting with the nurse. I told him how a specialist finally came in, by accident, because he overhead me complaining and that's how Truth got diagnosed. I also told him about the last two days – how he was getting better. How all the doctors were saying he would survive. How he walked the last day. But then I remembered something the nurse said to me the day before he died. Gerry, a male nurse, was one that I liked and had requested. The constant turnover of new nurses always stressed me out. Gerry came up to me in the hall on Sunday: "Does your husband do any drugs?"

"What? No. An occasional joint – like once or twice a month." I was honest about this. I actually wished he would smoke pot more as it calmed him down. "That's it. No alcohol. Why are you asking me this?"

"Oh because I keep upping his morphine and he's still in pain. I almost thought I gave him too much." the nurse said.

I can't believe he actually confessed that too me. Shit. I was so stressed at the time, it hadn't seemed important. I had forgotten all about it.

"I want to know more, Don. I need to know more about what happened – why he died." I said.

He was supposed to be getting better. I had to know what happened. What I didn't tell Don was that in the very back of my head I wondered if Truth had been white would all of this had happened? It was too late; I had gone there. Would he have gotten better treatment? He certainly didn't look like any of the other patients on that floor. I couldn't bring myself to say this, and certainly I didn't think we could prove this, but the thought remained in my head. It was a thought that I did not know what to do with. I didn't even want to have the thought, but it was too late.

My dad supported my decision to go see Don. He was also convinced that the care Truth received at the hospital was negligent. He wanted to tell his side of the story of the times he spent there alone with Truth. What he saw and heard. That morning, I had begun to read my father's handwritten account of that last night when Truth died, but I could not finish it. I made a photocopy and told myself I would read it one day. He was not alone, I kept telling myself. He did not die alone. My dad was there, the most loving man I know, holding his hand. My eyes began to tear up again thinking about it while seating across from Don's giant mahogany desk.

Don looked down at all the papers I brought him. A stack of about 300 pages, his entire medical chart that I had picked up earlier in the day, his death certificate, my dad and my written accounts of everything we experienced during the hospital stay and the autopsy report.

"Do you have the rest of this autopsy report?"

"No, that's all he gave me. Why what's missing?"

"There is no toxicology report here. We need to see what drugs were in his body when he died. Robert, call up this doctor and find out where the toxicology report is."

"From what you've told me, I think we have enough to look into this matter. But I need to warn you it will not be easy. Here in Nevada, before you can file a malpractice suit, you have to bring your case in front of the Medical Review panel. This is a group made up of roughly six people, two doctors, two lawyers and two appointed business people from the community. The intention is to catch frivolous lawsuits before they go to court. This review panel is highly slanted towards the doctors. And if we lose in front of them, our chances become very slim to win in a court case. But you never know, you will make a very sympathetic witness. If the panel decides in our favor, we can use that as evidence in our case, which goes a long way. It's going to be a long ride; these cases can be delayed for many years. The defendants, whoever we decide to name, will make sure of that. They'll try to keep delaying until you run out of money or until they wear you down."

He continued flipping through the medical chart. "And this could also get ugly; their lawyers could potentially begin looking at you and your husband when he was alive. Your character, what kind of people you were. They could potentially hire a private investigator to watch you, to see if you're dating. I'm not saying that will happen, but I have heard of it. We're talking wrongful death and medical malpractice, the stakes are high."

Our character? What difference does that make? Do I have to tell him we ran porn sites? I couldn't believe he was talking about me dating. I just lost my husband two weeks ago. What the fuck was he talking about?

"Don, I'm leaving for New Orleans tomorrow. I don't care what they do. I just want to know what happened."

Robert, shaking his head, walked into the room: "No toxicology report was run. The guy said nobody told him you needed one."

"That's not true" my dad piped up. "When the nurse came, I asked her if I needed to tell them any details about his case. She said no, they knew to do everything."

His body was already in the ground. We would never know how much of the drugs and painkillers were in his body that last day.

"We'll just have to build a case without it." Don proclaimed not showing any of the anger I was feeling.

Of course they didn't run one. It just added to my distaste for this place. A wasteland. I became more certain that this lawsuit was the right decision.

"Now we just need to talk about finances." Don continued.

I agreed to pay Don $2500 to start the case. He would send the records to a doctor that he knew who gave expert opinions. If this doctor agreed there was a case, Don would cover the rest of the costs in return for 35% of any judgments. I wrote Don a check, and shook his hand. I was convinced that this was the way for me to find out what really happened. And in finding out the truth, it would give me some comfort, some sense of peace. And besides I told myself, Truth would have wanted this. "Sue the mother fuckers," he would say, "No mercy."

Twenty

The next day, the moving company my father helped me locate, came in with a dozen men and packed up our entire house in one day, loaded it on a huge truck and headed off to New Orleans. I did not have the energy to lift a finger to pack one thing. My father and I hopped on a flight. I wanted to get out of Las Vegas as soon as possible. The only hesitation I had was the lingering feeling that Truth might come back, like he had been lost all this time, and he would come back to our house. Find it empty and me gone.

I did not leave you. I did not leave you, I said to the air as I sat in the aisle seat of the plane.

On November 1st, I settled into the guest bedroom in my parent's house – the same one I had been in when Truth and I first moved back. I spent most of my time alone in my room sleeping. My parents gave me all the space that I needed. No one expected anything from me.

I woke up and looked at my watch. It was now the ninth of November – twenty-nine days after Truth died. I kept track of how many days since he died. Died. Everything felt very strange, surreal. I sat down at the table in one of the two spare bedrooms of my parent's home. It was my father's makeshift office. I had deposited ten of our eighteen computers in this room. Their resting place while I figured out what to do with them. We had named all of our computers. Truth's main computer was Papa, and that's what I plugged in.

I had spent the past two weeks sleeping and reading, and now I was awake enough to begin thinking. Freedom gave me the room to think and for the first time, to question. Questions had lurked deep in my consciousness for many years. But these questions were not safe to come out. Until now.

Who are you? Or were you? Or are you? For now I'd try to figure out "were you". I went to Yahoo and typed in private investigators. A flurry of ads came up on the screen.

The stories Truth told me, early in our courtship, came back to me.

I came back from Grenada. I had only been back in the States a couple of weeks, I probably had posttraumatic stress syndrome. Kathy and I were in burger joint. Some guy said some racist thing about she and I being together. I start beating him. I couldn't remember the rest. But later I found out he died. During the trial, I would not show remorse. They convicted me and I was sent to Pelican Bay. It's one of the worst prisons in America. It's where the worst of the worst go – the men who kill other men in prison. They sent me there. I spent two years there and much of it in solitary confinement. When I came out someone from the NSA came to me. And offered me a job. They gave me a second Social Security number and I began working for them.

I looked at a few PI websites and settled on one: Advanced Research, Incorporated. I filled out the online form. Name, social security number, driver's license, birthdate, last known address, telephone number. I selected the report: Criminal record of all known misdemeanors and felonies in Alameda or Contra Costa for past twenty years, I selected delivery method: FedEx Overnight. I entered my credit card information and hit send.

I opened up a phone book and looked up Armed forces. I found an office not far from my parent's house. I grabbed a card from Truth's wallet, an Army ID card that had apparently gone through the washing machine more than once. His picture was torn out of it, but his name and birthdate were there: Paul Lewis, 1.14.62. I put the card in my wallet and drove to the office.

I sat in the waiting room for five minutes and then a man in uniform came out to greet me. He welcomed me into his office.

"Hi, my husband, my late husband, he was in the Army. Here's his ID. I wanted to find out how I can get a record of his military service and combat history."

I handed him the faded card. He took the card and glanced at it for a second handing it back to me.

"Ma'am, well I'm sorry to hear that your husband passed, but I'm afraid I can't help you with that. We're a U.S. Marine Corp recruiting office here. We don't deal with personnel records."

"Who would?"

"You're gonna want to call the National Personnel Records Office. I believe you could find that number on the Army website."

"Of course. Thank you."

It was almost five o'clock and no one would be around to receive my calls. I got into my car feeling stupid, as I pulled out clearly seeing US MARINES RECRUITING in big red letters on the window.

WHO ARE YOU? I screamed aloud in my car. Are you just a liar? Is that all you did to me the whole time - LIE?

A wave hit me and I began to sob. I want to know you. It felt so strange to be in the car driving without him there. He had always been with me, or I had always been with him, I'm not sure which. We were never apart. I looked to my right and he was not there. I reached over to the passenger seat and began punching the air. Who were you? Tell me who you are.

The next morning I began making phone calls to Army offices. After being redirected and told to call other offices, I finally found a woman who could help me. She was sending a form to fill out to request his record. I tracked the FedEx package and it said "delivered". I ran downstairs and found it on the slate floor under the mail slot. I ran back upstairs to my dad's office and shut the door behind me. I unzipped the envelope and removed three pages. First a cover letter, a copy of the invoice and on the last page the results.

The results page listed the details of the report that was run, listed Paul Lewis and his birthdate. Two big stamps marked CLEAR were printed on the page: No Records found.

I was not surprised. But I was angry.

I put my head down on the desk. Was I the most gullible woman on earth? Why would he lie? Did he want my sympathy? And was there any truth at all to what he told me? About anything?

Truth = Truth = hypocrite.

I knew where I could get more answers, but I wasn't quite ready to do it.

I made a list of all the questions I had about Truth:

    1.   Did he work for the NSA?

    2.   Did he work for the U.S. Embassy in France?

3. Did he go to Pelican Bay for two years?
4. How long was he in the Army?
5. Did he serve in the Airborne 82nd in Grenada and Nicaragua?
6. Did he have two SS numbers?
7. What does the writing in code in his notebook mean?

I began doing more research on the computer. The conflict in Grenada was in 1983 when he was twenty-one. The 82nd airborne was in Grenada. But Pelican Bay did not open its doors until 1989. I ran a search for his Social Security number, and it showed that it was issued in California in 1977. He would have been fifteen. It's not unusual to wait to send off for a child's social security number, I think. But if the NSA had issued him a second one then it would have been when he was much older. Maybe he had a second one he didn't tell me about. I opened up the brown notebook and looked at the pages upon pages of signs and symbols of some kind. Was it encrypted code? It didn't look like any language I knew. I considered how I could find someone to look at it for me and tell what it means – if anything.

I put all my records and paperwork into a folder and placed it into our fire-proof business safe that I had in the corner of the room. Sorry, *my* fireproof business safe. My family knew nothing about this. That was the way I wanted to keep it. To tell my parents now would cause them unnecessary stress. The drama was over. He was dead, and I was not stuck anymore. I could take care of myself. I slowly rotated the dial, hearing each click as it turned.

The papers were now locked away. My emotions, however, were not so easily hidden.

It probably is all made up, Amy. Garbage – all in his imagination. I began removing the thin layers of denial in my mind that I had any idea who this man was. What difference does it bloody well make? He is gone. The tears, my everyday playmates, came up knocking on my eyeballs. Deep breaths, Amy.

Twenty-one

Every single item that you buy in life, that outlives you, someone, some person, has to deal with. Has to pack, has to decide what to do with: to sell, to donate, to throw away? If you sell it you have to decide how much to sell it for, maybe even research what similar items go for; you have to advertise, you have to exchange money, maybe even make change. If you donate you have to pack up, decide what charity or friend to give it to, usually you have to bring it to them or arrange to be home when they come by. You have to make sure it works because you don't want to donate something that is broken. If you throw it away you have to lug it, schlep it to a waste bin and if it's a lot of things to a dumpsite. You don't think about this when you have money in your pocket and want things.

Every item in our Vegas house had a memory connected to it. Now I had to decide what to do with them all. I rented a huge storage space close to my parent's house. It was almost as big as our first tiny slum apartment. All of our stuff had been deposited there.

The week after he died, I had gone into our walk-in closet in Vegas and sniffed every item of his clothing, removing those pieces that still had his scent and packaging them into gallon size vacuum packed Ziploc bags. I imagined this was a new use for Ziploc bags they probably never advertised: preserving the scent of the dead. I would have taken his clothes in the dirty laundry basket, but my father had washed them. I cried when I found him in the laundry room trying to be helpful. I put the zip locked bags of clothes under my bed in my parent's guest bedroom.

I spent about two weeks going daily to the storage facility and sorting through stuff. I wanted to send some of his personal items to his daughters and Barbara. Tessa and Allison barely knew their dad. I barely knew their dad; the thought was now settling into me. He had neglected his duties as a father since the divorce, a fact I did know. I met them for the first time at the funeral. I looked through some of his watches. God, he loved watches – big, bulky silver expensive time pieces. Why he needed so many I don't know – always trying to outrun time I suppose. I picked out two watches and two of his leather jackets, and I put them in my car to send to his girls.

What the hell was I going to do with all this junk? That's all it was to me now, junk. I pulled the door shut as my stomach turned queasy. The smell of him, of us, of our life together was everywhere. His cigarettes permeated everything piercing through the boxes and into the air around me. I looked over at my empty car. I was in charge now.

Deep breaths.

I drove home and made a list.

The items that I had to keep: his clothes that still smelled of him, the contents of his bedside drawer, wallet, chain that connected his wallet to his pants, his piercing kit, his notebooks, a knapsack, his brown corduroy jacket, the extra programs from the funeral, the rose I had pressed that he gave me some time back, the champagne we never drank from when we got married, letters from him, cards, what few pictures we had. I counted them – only twenty-three photos with him in it, and one video. Remembering was not something high on our agenda. I took what I had and went to Walgreens and scanned the photos making copies in case I lost the originals. Then I made copies of the copies in case I lost those. I blew the best ones up to 8 x 10 which I put all over my room.

I created an altar on the dresser in my bedroom. This dresser happened to be the one from my old room as a child. I put up six different frames with pictures of Truth and us together surrounded by candles and a rosary I had bought in the hospital. I felt God was okay with me taking from whatever religious traditions gave me solace. I liked holding things when I prayed.

I wrote down what business equipment I would need to keep to run the websites that were generating an income. Since I wasn't hosting websites anymore, most of the servers, routers and networking equipment could be sold. I listed all the big ticket computer and electronic items that would sell for five hundred and above and advertised them on EBay.

I kept the furniture I knew I would use on my own. The rest was put into the largest Garage Sale that Timberlane Subdivision had ever seen. They also had "No Garage sales" in their neighborhood charter, so my Dad jokingly said he'd play lookout to the snob police patrolling the street as a small mass gathered waiting to get into my parent's backyard just before 8 am on a Saturday Morning. I tried to make it a festive occasion, serving sodas and beer and putting up brightly colored flags leading the way to the sale that covered almost half of the half-acre yard. I did not advertise it as an estate sale, nor that I was selling possessions of the recently deceased. For two days the garage sale ran and enough was leftover that I would later have two more garage sales.

"Will you take five dollars for this?" asked the large woman in red t-shirt with the ladder marked ten dollars in her hand.

"Yes"

"Will you take twenty for this?" asked the man in grey with the fifty-dollar VCR.

"Yes"

I think there is an unwritten rule at garage sales. You can't go too low or risk insulting the owner. Little did this crowd know I would have sold most everything for $1.

"Yes. Yes. Yes. Yes."

With each yes I felt lighter. With each yes I felt a little more oxygen in my lungs.

"Yes, of course you can have that jig saw for ten. Thank you." I smiled.

And breathed in and out and wondered what I would do next.

Twenty-two

There are certain advantages to being a widow. As a trade-off they are certainly not worth it, but from one who always searches for the silver lining, they are worth mentioning. I sat on the front steps of a run-down Creole cottage, the location of a weekly widow's group I joined, and talked to Jim, who had lost his wife to cancer two years ago.

"In the weeks and months after her death, I experienced a sense of clarity about life unlike anything I had ever known. The lucidity is mixed in with the shock and grief and craziness of the process, but it is not insanity. This gift is true wisdom. But know this. It fades with time. So use it. Use it before it goes away."

There were other advantages as well and many in my group reported the same experiences:

Weight loss: Food held little interest or taste for me, and the pounds miraculously began to melt off of me with no effort on my part.

The W Retort: The cards, wishes, and calls from loved ones came and then after the first month mostly went away. But I was quick to use the W word whenever I needed it or wanted it to protect me. "Hey my husband just died, get out of my face". "I can't possibly deal with your two hundred thousand dollar bill" I told the hospital administrator on the phone. "I was just widowed, you know, thanks to your incompetent doctors." It was just an insurance billing error they later said. I managed to get about six grand in late tax penalties removed with a finely crafted letter to the IRS utilizing the W word. The distinction of young W even more effective.

Fearlessness: Best of all, I simply wasn't afraid of the things that normally I would be. In fact, nothing seemed to scare me. The typical "bad day" went undistinguished against the backdrop of the worst year of my life. Washing machine breaks shooting out suds that flood the laundry room? Que sera sera. You want to rob me? Ok. You want to audit me. Be my guest. You want to shoot me? That looks just like my husband's gun. Oh my dead husband, he just died. Let me see that thing. I want to touch it.

In the first three months, I cycled between states of unbearable sadness, confusion and anger. The pain smashed into me in waves. I felt reasonably normal and then reality would hit. Most days still felt like a dream state. This can't be happening. This didn't just happen. A huge sense of incredulousness hung over me like the first time Truth struck me. Oh no you did not just hit me. Oh no you did not just get sick on me and die.

Who are you? And where are you? I missed his touch. How big and muscular his hands were. I missed his ear-to-ear grin and his smell and his face and his laugh and his skin and his tattoos and the way he greeted me each morning: Good morning Mrs. Lewis. I missed how secure I felt with him as CEO of our business. But, I didn't miss his moods, his fist, his threats, his guns, his jealousy, and his complete domination over me. Day to day life was easier for me as a widow; that I could not deny.

It was two weeks before the end of the millennium. Truth and I had made big plans for New Years on the strip.

I picked up the phone and dialed.

"Hello Kathy? You don't know me. My name is Amy. Truth … Paul's wife."

"Hi. I'm so glad you called. Tessa and Allison said … well I just wanted to thank you for being so good to them. You didn't have to. How are you? I can't even imagine what you must be … It was such a shock."

"I'm ok. I ahhh … I wanted to ask you a few things … about Paul and you." There was a slight pause where neither of us spoke. I took a quick breath gathering my courage …

"Yes he did."

"What?"

"What you were going to ask me."

"I don't know what you mean." But I did know.

"Oh I'm sorry I thought … never mind." She was quiet.

"That's not really why I called. Was he ever in Pelican Bay? Did he spend any time in prison?"

"No not while we were together. We did have this thing in the early eighties I think it was. He was accused of this robbery. He didn't do it. The guy said he looked like … it was ridiculous. He was exonerated."

"Yeah I heard that story. But nothing else? He was in Grenada or Nicaragua right? Those wars."

"Amy … No … I'm sorry. Not that I'm aware of."

"Oh okay." There was an awkward silence.

"Look I really appreciate what you're doing with the girls."

"I'm sorry I can't do more. I gotta go."

I hung up the phone quickly. Was I not the stupidest woman on the face of the earth? If there was an award for stupid, silly women, I would have won it. A loud yelp escaped – not quite a scream but a leaking of some voice I had never heard before that resided inside me. What was I thinking? And a new wave of pain and confusion hit me.

Did I even know anything about this man I lived with for so many years? Was everything I knew about him a lie?

1. Did he work for the NSA?

2. Did he work for the U.S. Embassy in France?

3. Did he go to Pelican Bay for two years?

4. How long was he in the Army?

5. Did he serve in the Airborne 82nd in Grenada and Nicaragua?

6. Did he have two SS numbers?

7. What does the writing in code in his notebook mean?

Truth = ? = dead

After my call to Kathy, and after receiving word from the U.S. Army that they had no record of Paul Lewis ever being in the Army, I came to the conclusion that I had no idea who I was married to. I had no idea if anything he ever told me was true. Probably, it began to sink in slowly; probably none of it was true. And I would never know.

I wasn't a smart, independent woman. I didn't know what I was doing. I remember the psychological evaluation I received in the hospital at nineteen; there was a line in her report: *Much of the insight she appears to have achieved may well be faulty, and it might well be time for her to turn her attention away from self-absorption and self-pity to healing and reparative strategies.* Maybe she was right.

I was fragile. I was naïve – stupid even – hell incredibly stupid some might say – but I also loved him. Despite everything, I loved him. Did that make me stupid or smart? Did my innocence protect me or did it cause all this pain? I know how to love. I can see light in everybody. I know how to suffer but also to love. Suddenly the question of love became important to me. But for once, it was the question of how to love me. For the first time, I was beginning to see that the only problem I needed to worry about is *how do I give myself the same love I gave him?* I let go of the mystery surrounding Truth's past and started focusing on my own.

From eighteen to twenty-three years old, I was on and off Paxil, Zoloft, Prozac, Celexa, and Trilafon. In the hospital, when drugs weren't enough, they had considered giving me ECT – a decision that thankfully was not acted on. The drugs had all helped to some small degree, at a cost that at the time seemed worth it, the cost being that the pills numbed me. And when all you feel is awful, not feeling much is an improvement.

But this time around, I was dead-set against drugs. I wanted to feel *everything*. I wanted to release every last pent up emotion from my body.

A month after returning to New Orleans I began seeing a therapist twice a week, Ben Phillips, whom I had seen at the age of seventeen. I trusted him deeply and he was the only counselor I had ever been able to work with. I was rarely attracted to white men and certainly not white men from the south, but Ben was an exception. He was intelligent, dignified, gentle – genteel even – and I was very attracted to him. I felt I had fallen deeply in love with him as a teenager, which he knew. Not an uncommon occurrence in therapy, it's called transference and when handled properly can be very useful to the therapeutic relationship. It had run its course with the most respectful and proper behavior on his part, and I was left with a feeling of love, respect and fondness for him. I had not warmed to most of the therapists I had seen in college; I held either apathy or outright distaste for them. I had kept in touch with Ben after I left for Berkeley, and he was the first person that I opened up to when I returned home.

I had never known that Ben had lost his wife to cancer when he was in his early thirties. He had long since remarried. He understood grief, and he patiently sat witness to my process.

I read a lot about grieving. I conducted my own scientific in-quiry, reading journal articles searching for acknowledgement and understanding. I found myself drawn to work from the "death awareness movement", which stressed death, dying and bereave-ment as meaningful human experiences beyond their medical context. Out of this movement, the term "grief work" was coined. The researchers saw grief as an active process. So time itself would not heal my wounds, it's what I did with the time that would make the difference.

This grieving business did feel like work to me, my new full time job. I became particularly interested in the work of Colin Murray Parkes, a British Psychiatrist. He wrote about grief being a process of "reconstructing normal". I learned that I had to reconcile my reality that existed before Truth died with my new reality. I needed to regain the feeling that my life was normal again. My grief was "complicated", as the experts call it, by the fact that my life before Truth died was anything but normal. And while my life now didn't feel normal, it felt a lot better than before he died. I experienced guilt about this, but I could not deny it. My life *was* easier. No one was yelling at me, controlling the hell out of me, threatening to kill me, hitting me, and keeping me from being happy. And for the first time in my life, that included me.

And then there was the gnawing feeling that had arrived in the hospital and had grown stronger since Truth died. I didn't know what it meant, and a feeling this strong, appearing out of nowhere, appearing connected to nothing was strange. It was the feeling of not being alone, even when I'm alone, the feeling of a child cradled at her mother's breast, safe and protected. The feeling remained, and I didn't know what to do with it.

I didn't walk around like a Pollyanna, spouting this. Most of the time, I was catatonic at worst, a hopeful mopey at best. That's what it looked like from the outside. But if I stopped for a minute and let this feeling of safety and protection in, if I opened the door to my heart just a smidgen, my sadness and confusion disappeared. When I was up for it, I let it spray itself all over me like my favorite new exotic fragrance.

A widower in my Tuesday night group walked to my car with me one night after group. He had been a widower for over a year. "During the first year you will feel closer to Heaven than you ever have - or ever will again." He was right. It had to be Heaven. It had to be God. Who else would it be?

My room looked like a tribute to St. Truth. Photos everywhere, mementos on makeshift altars that I kissed and catered to daily. My therapy sessions were something else entirely. I learned quickly that it's tricky staying mad at a dead man. And it was even harder to express my rage to my dead husband. I spent a lot of time in my sessions trying.

"I hate him … I want him right here in my face I want to tell him to his face – you mother fucker – you had no right – no right to terrorize me. I want to torture him. Make him feel what I did. And then I want him to tell me he still loves me. Tell me you love me after I point a gun in your face!"

"So tell him all that," Ben would say.

I looked over at Ben and rolled my eyes.

"I can't … what difference does it make. He's not here. He's not gonna be here. It's no use."

"You said yourself you still feel him around you."

"But that's different. I can't … I can't like yell at a spirit. What's the use?"

"Tell me then – pretend I'm him when he was alive."

"If you were him alive, I wouldn't be here and I sure as hell wouldn't be telling him how angry I was. He would kill me. That's the problem. He would kill me. I couldn't get angry. That was his department."

"I said pretend."

"I don't want to pretend. It's useless. It's fucking useless. It's over and I don't hate him. That's the problem. No matter how much I want to I can't hate him. I can't. I wish I could hate him." I began to cry. All I could do these days was cry.

"I just wish he was here … I didn't get to say goodbye." I rested my forehead on my hands my palms pressing into my eyeballs. Everything hurt. Every pore hurt. I picked up a Kleenex and wiped my wet mascara eyes.

"I love him. I hated all the control but I love him. I don't know how I can still love someone but at the same time hate him. I'm such an idiot."

"Fuck!" Frustrated I belted out some kind of strange half yell, half cry with the snotty Kleenex crumpled tightly in my fist. I sat with my knees brought up to my chest as I breathed heavily with the mucus making croaky sounds in my nasal cavity.

Doing good work in therapy is rarely pretty. At first, releasing emotions locked beneath the surface through words and sounds rather than through blood felt clumsy and ineffectual. Ben patiently sat witness. He supported me knowing exactly when to push and when to let me do the work I knew I had to do. He knew my modus operandi and let me release my pent up energy and rage. I was a woman with a lot that needed to come out safely.

"It's a lot easier loving him knowing he's not here to make my life hell anymore."

"I know."

"You know he was the one who got me to stop cutting. How many years did I do that shit?"

For weeks I flip-flopped from one extreme to the other, screaming one minute, crying the next, cursing him in the living and calling out to him in the hereafter. I wanted to go wherever my grief took me and let it all out. For once, I wasn't afraid. Now nothing scared me. I felt guided, and felt I was allowed to reconnect with the light that had always been there inside me.

Christmas 1999 came and went, and I remembered little of it. I had few responsibilities and I loved that. I chose that. I worked about fifteen hours a week maintaining the websites. The rest of the time was spent on me. Doing whatever the hell I wanted to. After four and half years allowing myself to be dominated, I had some time to make up for. I was learning to take care of myself. I started to run again.

Running was the only activity that was one hundred percent guaranteed to get me out of my head – to get me out of whatever funk I had gotten into. It was my medicine, my meditation and my peace. I stopped running during my relationship with Truth because he wasn't a runner and my leaving the house to run by myself – well, it upset him. It was the first thing I resented him for. And that resentment ran deep. But I chose to stop. I chose to keep the peace. I chose to give away myself. To forget about myself. To disregard myself. For what, I wonder? I look back and wonder, for what? Was the love that great? No. Of course not. Am I an idiot? No. Low self-esteem. Yes, I think we're getting closer. But I'm not completely satisfied with that answer.

Starting to run when you've gained almost a hundred pounds posed its challenges. I didn't care. The thought of people staring at my fat ass running, which might have kept me from going in the past, meant absolutely nothing to me now. I started slow. I drove to Audubon Park. I ran about fifty yards and then walked. Then ran fifty yards then walked. My ego was the most sore as it remembered how fast and good I used to be when I was a kid. But I also knew how to train, and that nothing happens overnight. I gradually increased. I hired a personal trainer, and I stopped stuffing everything under the sun into my mouth. The weight slid off me.

My sister had invited me to a New Year's Eve party at Anne Rice's house. Normally I would have jumped at the chance to meet an author I loved, but the thought of getting dressed up, making myself look presentable, and socializing, counting down, pretending to be happy about this passage of time was just too much. I stayed in bed.

I was fast asleep as the new millennium made itself known. My year 2000 bug had struck two months and twenty days early.

Future was not something I was going to deal with just yet. I made a conscious decision to live without time for as long as it took for me to deal with this grief thing, this reconstructing normal. I had no expectations, put no pressure on myself, and did not think or worry about the future. I allowed myself to be. To be. What a brilliant concept. I had never considered giving myself that option before. I always had to *be* something. It was always something other than what I was. Just being. Given all that had happened, being was about all I could do. And for the first time in my life, being seemed like enough.

I decided I wanted to *be* on my own. So that's what I did. Even though I had spent copious amounts of time alone at my parent's house, I craved more solitude and independence. I craved a space of my own to emote in, to grow into whatever the hell I was going to grow into. I was like a mama cat looking for a quiet spot to give birth in – except I was giving birth to me.

Twenty-three

A few days after the New Year, I moved into a one hundred and fifty year old house on Dauphine, in the heart of the French Quarter, to an apartment that was the second and third floors of a traditional three-bay, three-story townhouse. The Creole townhouses took shape after fires of 1788 and 1794 burned down the town's freestanding French Colonial houses. The Quarter is the historical heart of the city, a rectangle of roughly ten by thirteen blocks, the original settlement of New Orleans, a mixture of French, Spanish and Creole architecture. On the main floor, I walked into an expansive living room with crown moldings, a large glass chandelier, refinished oak floors, exposed brick walls and twelve-foot ceilings. In front was another large room with the original fireplace and a balcony enclosed by delicate wrought iron that looked onto Dauphine Street; I used this room as my office. There was a small, refinished galley kitchen that looked out over the courtyard where the former slave quarters were rented out to vacationers. I could not fathom how the tiny buildings that used to house human slaves had become fashionable to rent out as a pied-a-terre to wealthy (mostly white) vacationers. If I were in charge of the city, I would burn them all down – or at the least make them into museums or art galleries of African art. I put up some blinds blocking its view from the kitchen; it was the only part of the house I didn't love.

The entire third floor was a huge attic bedroom. Despite the roof pitch, the attic ceilings were still about ten feet tall and the attic was over five hundred square feet. It was a bedroom to start over in, a beautiful room of my own in which to grieve and heal. It looked out over a cement play yard for the Catholic school next door. This house had one hundred and fifty years of life in it, and I expect, a hundred fifty years of death. This was a house that spirits would come back to. You could just sense it. There were many urban tales of hauntings all over the French Quarter, and every night the tourist tours in horse drawn carriages stopped on of this block and told ghost tales.

My place was only one block off of Bourbon Street, in the gay area of the Quarter. Sunday night was Broadway night at the bar on Dauphine and St. Ann, and I would sit on my balcony listening to show tunes sung with wild abandon. I could walk out of my house and I could lose myself in the drunken revelry. Or I could go and spend hours in and out of the art galleries and antique stores of Royal Street. I had my choice of more bars per square block than any city in the world, many open twenty-four hours a day, seven days a week. Bars that you could find drinking companions at six am on a Tuesday morning. I had taken to drinking a bit. There were more than a few mornings when I had a shot of tequila with my corn flakes. I allowed myself such indulgences without judgment. Another perk of widowhood. Oh you think I'm drinking too much – well, honey, I think I'm entitled – I was abused and now I'm widowed, and I'm still only 27. Entitlement, some days, was my only friend.

My favorite bar was Lafitte's Blacksmith Shoppe, around the corner from my house. It was the oldest structure in the Quarter, built sometime in the 1700's. It was always dark inside, lit only by candles and a piano man in the back sang happy sing-along songs, with the occasional sad one thrown in for good measure. But since food was always my first love, the drinking became only a diversion, never a problem. I did what I needed to do to get through the days. I roamed a lot. The air was thick with life, thick with death, thick with eternity. I sensed the thousands who had walked these same alleys grieving as I was. Reconstructing normal. Finding themselves.

I read. I wrote. I walked. I worked out. I worked the bare minimum to upkeep the porn sites and continue generating income. And I went to the movies. I saw just about every movie that hit the theaters the year after Truth died. Good (Gladiator), bad (Deuce Bigalow, Male Gigalo), really bad (Coyote Ugly), big budget (Charlie's Angels), low budget (Girlfight), foreign (Crouching Tiger, Hidden Dragon) – the only requirement was that it didn't feature any black men in hospital beds (Bone Collector was therefore out of the question despite my liking Denzel & Angelina). I went almost every night to the movies - always by myself. I had to be alone. I wanted the freedom that comes from solitude – I could cry unexpectedly, laugh inappropriately, talk out loud to my dead husband, which I did all the time. I didn't want to explain my quirks to anyone. I didn't want anyone feeling sorry for me. I went to the movies so much the box office workers got to know me, and on Friday and Saturday date nights, when shows would sell out, they'd let me in anyway. You can almost always find a single open seat - an advantage of flying solo.

During the day I could occupy myself, but nights after I got out of the movie were the hardest. Before getting into bed, I would pray at my altar in my attic bedroom and talk to Truth. *Where are you? I know you're out there. I miss you.*

I kissed each picture on the altar and blew out the candles, and I went to sleep to a local New Orleans music video channel. It played videos like MTV but they were mostly Southern rap artists, young black urban men like the Cash money guys before they got really big. It comforted me to fall asleep to them. They reminded me of Truth – their rage, drive, boldness, and the way they excited me. I drifted off to sleep to the sounds of their bling – sleep that would take me to the most amazing places very soon.

Twenty-four

In the first six months I had a lot of dreams about Truth coming back to life. He'd return ready to resume his life with me, and I had to explain that the business was gone. He'd get angry and I'd wake up terrified; it took me a while to remember that he was not coming back, that I didn't have to be afraid.

I had decided to let a lot of the business go. I kept one site as my single revenue stream. About six months before Truth died, I had started a new adult site and insisted I be the one to do everything from scratch. Truth laughed at the thought of me doing it all by myself, and he let me try on my own for a few weeks, before coming in and offering his help. By then, I knew I needed the assistance. It was my creative brainchild, a site exploring the eroticism of natural redheads. I made the decision to keep and run All Redheads and sell off everything else. The redhead site did very well but still the income was less than half of what we used to make. It didn't matter; my lifestyle was not nearly as extravagant, so I had more than enough to live comfortably. The business had been such a huge source of pride for Truth – for us both. I felt guilty for letting so much of it die; for not wanting it to grow. My greatest fear was that Truth would come back to life, and I'd have to face his wrath about that. Or what I thought his wrath would be.

In early April, I was having one of those nights where I missed him intensely, viscerally. I didn't feel this way every night but sometimes I felt the pain in every bone of my body. I screamed out and cried furiously. On this particular night I missed being touched. I was so hungry and lonely for touch – physical contact. I had begun getting my nails done every week just so I could get the free hand massage. I cried myself into a deep sleep.

I am on a road with a large lake on the left hand side. It is dark and I am sitting alone in my car, a blue Mazda Miata with the top down. There is no one else on the street. Truth appears from where the water is and walks up to me in the car. He reaches out one finger and touches my bare shoulder.

I instantly woke and sat up, forced out of sleep by an intense sensation of electricity running through my body. I had been mildly electrocuted one night in college working at Larry Blakes. I'd been unplugging a lamp with a bad connector and felt a shock that almost knocked me over. It was exactly this feeling that ran through my body, forcing me out of sleep.

I knew quite a bit about dreams from years of therapy and was pretty adept at analyzing mine. I knew there were anxiety dreams like the ones where Truth came back to life and was mad at me. There were highly metaphorical process dreams that dealt with the deep undercurrents of my subconscious. I wrote my dreams down most every night and used them to guide me. I knew what a dream was – what it felt like.

I also knew what a dream wasn't, or should I say, when I was sleeping and something altogether undreamlike happened. I knew this *dream* wasn't coming from me. I didn't really know at the time that people called them *visits*. All I could tell was that this was no dream. This was real.

It sounded a little crazy, even to me. Dead husband touches me in my dream and I feel electric current and wake up and I'm thinking, I'm convinced this is ... what, a ghost? Yes, it's a ghost. No, I wasn't crazy. I was a lonely young widow, naïve, unstable with a history of mental problems. But *that* was not a dream.

In all of my dreams since he died, Truth was the man I knew: angry, intense and wanting things from me. But this time, the man in my dream who looked like Truth, I had *never* experienced *him* before. This Truth, had not one ounce, not one droplet, of negative in him. I didn't know him like that. I had never met him like that. It was like meeting him for the first time. Him but not the Truth I knew. It was so clear to me. This was how I first knew that he was visiting me from – well – from the afterlife. His soul, or whatever you want to call what survives death, had just touched me. So, the logic clicked into my brain, this means there is an afterlife. This was big. Big Big Bigger than I ...

He just touched me.

I sat up in the dark in my hundred and fifty year old attic bedroom and felt closer to God than I had ever before. I sat in a magical space where time did not try to fool me into believing he existed. Where I reached and touched eternity. Touched love. Touched forgiveness and touched healing and touched the infinity that tortured me as child. The forever and ever and all the "evers" were in a circle holding hands like children at recess. I began to cry, not out of fear or anger or grief but out of immeasurable gratitude and joy. A glorious thank you emanated from every pore in my body. I smiled the sweetest smiles through the tears and I sat alone and not alone and knowing I'd never be alone, feeling it in every pore of my body. I was not alone. And then I made love to myself, caressed every square inch of my body that I had been at war with since I was a young girl, and I drifted off into a delightful peaceful slumber.

Twenty-five

Not long after Truth died, I made an appointment for a group session with George Anderson on Long Island. I put myself on a six-month waiting list for a chance to spend a few hours in a group session with nine others. My date was nearing. George was one of the top mediums in the world. His abilities had been tested extensively. He was the only medium invited to Holland by Anne Frank's family. I don't know if he actually made contact with her. People in the know about such things called him the "Stradivarius among mediums". He had a number of books out, and I read about his life and work. A deeply religious man, he said he was a passive receiver of communication from spirits. He never called or conjured up spirits; they came to him, and he discerned them. He did not work through a spirit guide nor did he go into a trance. "Spirits are all around us existing as some form of energy," he said. For some reason, not all of us can communicate directly with them. George's "gift" allowed him to act as a sort of radio receiver through which the spirits communicated on an energy frequency that most of us were not consciously attuned to. He cannot control which spirits come through or how long the communication lasts. In other words, no money-back guarantees.

I packed my bags for my trip to New York to see George. I was excited and unsure of what to expect. The whole situation made me smile. I was flying hundreds of miles to meet a man who talks to dead people – who might be able to talk to my late husband. What would I say to him if he came through? Fuck you? You were a shitty husband to me. Had I now completely lost it? Was I just desperate? Did I even want to talk to him?

My plane arrived late in pouring rain. Would a spirit wait for a delayed flight? I jumped into a cab for the half hour drive to the hotel. I couldn't contain my excitement and told the taxi driver where I was going. She had no doubts that talking to dead people was most definitely possible, and she expertly sped in and out of traffic, a madwoman driving another madwoman late for an appointment with her dead husband. I had no time to check in; I ran into the hotel conference room, dropped my bags next to me, and plopped my butt down in the seat closest to George.

George sat up front and the chairs were arranged in a U shape around him. I sat at the very top of the right side of the U. There was one other single person, and the rest were couples. I got out my tape recorder and pressed play. Before we began, George gave instructions to only respond with yes or no and not to give him any more details.

Much to my surprise, Truth came through first. I had never met George Anderson, and he knew absolutely nothing about me beforehand. George tended to repeat himself, so I have included an edited version of the transcribed recording. There was some confusion in the beginning as it seems multiple spirits came in and were talking.

George: Well I have to start somewhere. A male presence comes up to you and embraces you with love.

Amy: Yes

George: Somebody talks about the younger male that's passed on. Do you understand?

Amy: Young … yeah.

George: Somebody is coming around you and the male presence that first came in and came up to you is talking about passing on young.

Amy: Yes

George: By the standard of the day, not ten years old. And he does call out to you as family so I take it that's true?

Amy: Yes

George: Now this is interesting, he speaks about his mother. Do you understand?

Amy: Yes

George: He says she's here. So I take it she's passed on?

Amy: Yes

George: Ok. So she must be the lady that's with him. Cause he's talking about his mother. And that she's here with me (pause) And, he comes as family to you but also comes in friendship. So I take it you and he were close?

Amy: Yeah.

George: Well certainly he feels close to you from the hereafter. (Pause)

Amy: Yeah

George: He claims he comes to you in dreams. He states it's not the first time you've heard from him. But again he embraces you in friendship so apparently you and he were friends as well as family members. (Pause) He also puts a big heart in front of you. Do you understand?

Amy: I understand.

George: (pause) This young male keeps kind of backing off and coming back … I think he's afraid he's confusing me.

Amy: (laugh)

George: And frankly at this moment he is. Because he's not coming out and saying how he's connected to you, which would break the ice for me but he comes to you as family.

I had read a lot about mediums and for many, it was not a direct conversational language that they had with the spirit. Often the medium has to interpret symbolic information that is put in their head as a thought from the spirit energy. So there seemed to be some confusion in the beginning between him and this spirit, who might be Truth.

George: He keeps telling me that you and he are linked. You understand?

Amy: (definitive) Uhuh

George: Cause that's what's confusing me. He keeps going like this in front of me and that means we're linked. (George linked his two fingers together in circles)

Amy: Right.

George: And again puts the big heart in front of you. So it must …

Amy: (starts to respond)

George: Don't say anything, But he wanted it to make sense because he's doing it over again.

Amy: It means something to me.

George: And frankly he's not the most patient guy in the world.

Amy: (laughs)

George: And to be honest with you neither am I … And he's losing his patience with me. And I'm, like, well, you're the one who's supposed to you know be coming forward, so step on it …

Amy: (laughs)

George: Cause he speaks of passing suddenly?

Amy: Yeah

George: And he says you won't be able to respond to this but he tells me that he knew he was going to pass on. Because he's not surprised to be where he is. And again the heart comes in front of you and he tells me he's your sweetheart. He did link with you again and then he said that you and he are one in the heart. So apparently he is your sweetheart.

Amy: Yes

George: Cause now he steps forward and claims …Yeah he steps forward and claims he's your husband. And I mean you look like a pretty young widow but I've had younger. And I can't help but laugh but he says to me the reason he's first is because he's impatient, he doesn't have the patience to wait.

Amy: (laughing)

George: So as soon as the opportunity opened … swoosh … he moved right in.

I was shocked when George said this. This was the inpatient, has-to-do-everything-in-a- hurry Truth I knew. Did his soul really maintain some of his personality even after leaving his body?

George: Cause your husband blesses you for being so good to him prior to his passing. And again states that he knew he was going to pass. You're shocked by his death, he says, but you're not shocked by his death. And he states you never want to give up hope. But, when the time comes, he says he passes very suddenly. He also apologizes for his passing particularly for what you have to go through. I don't know why but he wants it known that you did not fail him, do you understand? And as he states it's very important that you know that. He knows that you love him and he loves you. Because even towards the end he admits he was becoming a little distant? He puts an ice cube in front of you and says he might have seemed very cold. (pause) Now he speaks of family, do you understand?

Amy: Yeah

George: Yeah that's what I'm wondering ... he's speaking of family. So I'm assuming he's meaning yours and his or if he has his own family.

Amy: Yes (I assumed he was calling out to his daughters, Tessa and Allison, here.)

George: He's calling out to family. He also tells me this is the reason in the beginning he came through in friendship because he wants it understood that as much as you're husband and wife, you're still friends. Even if he might have seemed that he didn't want to be friends with you anymore. Cause he does state – and this is no reflection on you – he does say that he wasn't the happiest guy on earth. He's much happier where he is. (pause) He admits having a struggling time on earth, more so with himself. Because he keeps showing me lemons, which is a signal that he always felt like he was getting handed lemons. Things are not working out for him as expected.

Amy: Yes.

George: He spoke of a health problem … do you understand? But he also admits to being sick at heart. Which is usually I'm emotionally distressed too.

Amy: Yeah. I understand.

George: Also admits a little afraid to pass on. You know now that it's over with it's like walking from one room to the hallway. He says there's nothing to fear but fear itself. He also remembers a sense of resentment. You know when he knew he was going to pass on. Like you know life's been hard enough. But he keeps saying that he's back to his old self again and he does say you look for signs from him, but as he clearly states, sometimes you do get them and other times you're looking very hard and you don't think you're getting it. But as he says sometimes, when you look too hard, you're actually overlooking what's there. Yes he does talk about the illness sneaking up on him, yes? Because all of a sudden it's there.

Amy: Yes

George: Because when he said it before that it was a sudden passing, I was starting to think accident … and he said no no no don't go in the wrong direction. But, it's like the illness is there but you don't know it … and all of a sudden the symptoms appear and bingo it's taking its toll. You know up until that point he thought he was fine and healthy. If anything he said he felt tired. Yeah because he does admit at times kind of suffering in silence – he might not have felt well but was kind of keeping it to himself. It's not like he is the doctor type.

Amy: Yes

George: He wants you to understand that you could not save him. Because he knows that you think well gee if we had known sooner we could have done something about it and prevented this and he says you'll obsess out of fear that you should have been more receptive. But he says he didn't know so how could you know. You know he didn't feel well but still at the end he thought he was coming down with something (Pause) Hmmm this puzzles me … he talks about an explosion in the system … you understand?

Amy: Yes

George: Cause there's a volcanic eruption in front of you so apparently something is simmering like a volcano and then …

Amy: yes

George: It blows. (pause) He does say it affects the heart.

Amy: Yes

George: He tells me his heart explodes. So apparently he had some sort of massive coronary or whatever. (pause) Which is interesting he says has genetic connections.

I couldn't believe what I was hearing. The skeptic in me was sitting next to me analyzing everything. He just described very accurately the way his heart condition seemingly came out of nowhere, but it had been simmering inside of him without his knowledge. And literally the aorta going into his heart exploded – that is how he died. How could George know any of this? What are the statistical chances he could guess that?

George: Yeah he admits that where he's sick at heart - that's the emotional illness not that he was a nut case. It's just that he was extremely stressed out here, because over there he says it's like I'm on the vacation I never got. Where he can actually relax and sit back and he says there's no bull over there. So he doesn't have all the worries of that. He wants to let you know you're not alone but does strongly encourage you that you have to go on with your life. And it's not that he's being insensitive to your loss but as he states you don't have much choice in the matter. And one thing about your husband I think you could always depend on him to tell it like it is.

Amy: Yeah

George: Towards the end, did he seem like crabby? It wasn't like it was anything against you – you know how somebody doesn't feel well so they are a little on the grouchy side. He wasn't feeling well, but wasn't able to put his finger on it.

Amy: Right

George: Again he encourages you to go on with your life. He knows you feel like you didn't really have a chance to say goodbye to him. But as he states you don't have to because he has not left you – physically yes, but spiritually no. He jokes that you talk to him so you must believe he's still around you.

Amy: Yeah

George: That you sense he's there. But he does want to assure you that he still loves you and always has because there was tension building there on his part and you might have thought this thing was starting to go thumbs down. Again it felt like you were walking on eggshells. One minute everything is going swell and then all of a sudden you know it's like he's got a bug up his rear end or something … it's like what's causing this? And of course, you're naturally inclined to think am I doing something wrong, that things aren't right. And he says clear your head from that. It was just stress he tells me, not feeling well. It was just – I just feel like waves overpowering me so apparently he just felt over-whelmed.

Is he describing the violence? It sounded like that to me. Did I need an apology? I don't think so. I was mostly just looking for proof that this was really him. That was what I wanted.

George: He says you were certainly a joy in his life and still are. But he impresses you once again that you should not bury yourself alive. You are your own person and you have to go on with your life. You have a unique purpose here even though you don't see it. And he says we'll meet up again here someday, but he encourages you to go on with your life. He says he's very close to his mom in the hereafter so apparently they were close here on earth because it's almost like he never got over her loss. So the two of them are back together again.

Amy: Yes

George: And he says he wouldn't be there if he wasn't sup-posed to be there. (Pause) I just want you to strictly understand that. He also spoke of an anniversary understand?

Amy: Recently yeah

George: Because he keeps wishing you a happy anniversary. But also happy anniversary of our meeting.

Amy; Yeah. Yeah.

George: Because that one stands out more singularly than your actual on paper anniversary

Amy: Yeah

George: He says he's more celebrating the anniversary of your meeting because he says that's when cupid's arrow struck.

This one *really* got me. We did always celebrate the date of the first night we got together as our real anniversary. Our wedding anniversary had just passed about six weeks ago but it was something we barely celebrated. The real anniversary we celebrated was in May. How the hell could George know this kind of detail? My skeptic started coughing trying not to acknowledge what I was feeling in every bone in my body. A cheek-to-cheek grin broke out over my face, as goose bumps made my skins feel like it was vibrating.

George: Once again he calls out to his family. Before he also seemed to call the name Rich or Richard. Mean anything to you at all? He called out so it might have been somebody he knew. He spoke of you know a pretty good show up at his wake and funeral so it could have been anybody who came to pay their respects. Because that name and Diana came in too.

Diana was Truth's cousin that was closest to him. At the time, I had no idea who Richard was.

George: He does have a good sense of humor. He makes a joke of the fact that even he didn't realize that many people liked him – you know until he passed over and that many people showed up. Even though he could be grouchy, he definitely can be fun. So he does that purposefully. (Pause) Yes again he keeps putting a big heart in front of you. (Pause) All right, he tells me he's going to step aside so that somebody else can come through. He does like to talk though doesn't he? Probably a good thing that he did come in first. Not only for the lack of patience but also the fact that he likes to yak.

I stopped my tape recorder, and sat there trying to be calm and quiet out of respect for the other participants who had not had their turn, but trembling with awe and joy spilling out of my ears.

The truth was very important to me. What was true and what was not? Did what I felt just happened really happen? Did this man really just communicate with my late husband or was I falling prey to some sort of mind game or trick? Was he reading my mind? Was I a desperate fool? I did have a history of believing things that weren't true. While my skeptic had not completely shut up, I did not have any doubts after the reading. While not everything he said made sense to me, there were enough details he couldn't possibly know or guess to lead me to believe this was real. And if I still had doubts, they had disappeared after I sat and listened intently to eight other readings. I did not know these people or any of the details of their stories. But I didn't need to know the facts to be able to see the looks on their faces as George communicated with their loved ones on the other side. The look on their faces spoke for itself; it was probably the same look on my face. Time after time I witnessed the "dead" communicating with the living.

Four hours after I sat down in the chair, I rose and checked into the hotel and very quietly walked up to my room. I unlocked the door and walked over to the bed and lay down. I rested with arms and legs outstretched and eyes wide open. If I were paying attention to time, hours would have passed by. The dead communicating with the living. The dead? Dead? Communicating with the living. They were there. Truth was right there.

Everything I had ever learned about death was wrong. Everything I thought I knew was a lie.

All my assumptions about life had been built on the belief that death ends everything about us. If there is a part of us that goes on forever, everything now looked different. My world had just become a much gentler place. While these realizations had been dawning on me since the moment I saw Truth's dead body, now they had finally dropped into me full force. Dropped on top of me. Now I could not deny it. I couldn't lie to myself anymore. The girl who hated the world – who had tried to commit suicide – who used to gash into her skin and get excited by the blood dripping down – the girl who thought she knew everything – who thought she knew what was best. I really didn't know anything. I had it all wrong.

I stared at the ceiling with tears running and a silly grin that had been waiting for twenty-seven years to come out smashed over my face, grinning from head to toe, grinning from breast to breast, grinning through every layer of skin. I had it all wrong.

How could I hate myself? How could I hate myself so much? How could I hate my life? How could I hate my body? How could I hate anything? If I'm going to be here forever, then how can I hate anything?

I felt this tornado of relief rush over me, and blow away all of my hate, and all of my pain, and all of my fear. We don't really die. Truth did not really die. I will not really die. No one will ever really dic. The forever and ever of darkness that used to torture me had transformed into a forever and ever of light and love and peace. I felt like a walking talking billboard for born agains – an image that disgusted me, but only when I thought about it later. At this moment in time, I felt no disgust. All I could do was laugh. That's all that was left to do.

It had ALWAYS been this way. I just had it all wrong.

I eventually drifted off into a very sweet sleep with the grin on my face still in place when I awoke. I transcribed the tape recording and checked out of the hotel. I took a cab into the city and spent the next day enjoying myself in Manhattan. Enjoying my independence. Enjoying my lightness. Enjoying my glow. Enjoying my femaleness! I was free. Truth was at peace and we were connected forever. It was time for me. It was time for me to start loving myself, time for me to start sharing myself. Time for me to start living the life I was supposed to life, the life I that was waiting for me all along, waiting patiently for me to see clearly. As Truth's spirit said, *you have a unique purpose here even though you don't see it.* I skipped when I walked down Fifth Avenue. Skipped into the shops, to a show, to a cab, right on to the plane and off back home to New Orleans.

My Mom and Dad picked me up from the airport. I was glowing.

Twenty-six

Monday morning after returning from Long Island, I sashayed into Ben's office. He took a good hard look at me after I plopped myself down on his sofa. I couldn't stop grinning.

"So I take it the trip went well."

I grinned some more.

"Ben, he was there … I swear I am not crazy. He came in first … first … I was so worried I'd be the only one that wouldn't have someone come through – but he came in first because he didn't have the patience to wait, isn't that funny."

"Slow down … let me enjoy this." Ben was excited as I was. "What did he say?"

"He said he was ok. Happy. He talked about how he died. He said it was an explosion in the system, which it was -that's what the actual autopsy report said. And he actually mentioned people that were at his funeral – like names. There was Diana and then this name Richard; I didn't know who that was but I asked Barbara and she said it was a cousin from Seattle that Truth was close to when he was young. He was there at the funeral, I just didn't know it. And he wished me happy anniversary but Ben he said no, the anniversary of our meeting. Which is exactly what we celebrated. There's more … I taped it all and wrote it down. It was unfucking believable." I was trembling getting goose bumps as I talked.

"I mean what are the chances Ben – what is the likelihood that he could guess all that? Not likely. You know what freaked me out is that Truth still had some of his personality that he had here. He was actually getting impatient with the medium. Yeah. He said that. That's why he came in first and then there was some confusion and George actually said he's getting impatient with me. It's still unbelievable to me. Everything feels different to me now – softer."

"Your very essence looks different. Like your DNA has changed."

"Yeah, my spiritual DNA." I laughed.

I did feel different, as though my DNA was different. That trip changed something in me so deep, not only could it not be unchanged, but now everything I did felt easier, as if I had been fighting against some invisible force that was now gone. Yes, my very essence had changed. I felt lighter. I just smiled at Ben and enjoyed the feeling of being right with the world. I beamed. I had been at war with myself in one way or another my whole life – I was never good enough, pretty enough, skinny enough, never enough. I had gotten it somewhere into my brain that I was just bad. A bad seed – a bad girl guilty of so many things – but none that I could actually name but somehow needing to be punished. So I punished myself however I could, I cut into my skin, I ran myself into the ground, I ate myself sick, I let my husband beat me, terrorize me. I deserved it – or so I thought. Why? What the hell had I done? I think back as far back as I can think and I can't come up with one damn thing I've done that's so bad that it warrants one-hundredth of that pain. I don't know why I thought I deserved it. But that was over now. There wasn't even any scar tissue, it was as if it had never even happened. I had just woken up. Woken up to myself. Woken up with time finally on my side.

What was I going to do was now a question I could ask myself. I knew I couldn't stay a hermit in my French quarter hideaway for much longer, and suddenly I felt the need to talk, to share, and to open myself up. It was now seven months since Truth died. I was still counting, still praying and talking to him every night, still missing him intensely – but now there were periods of days at a time when I didn't miss him so much. The shock was all worn off now. I was used to being on my own. After my session with George, I felt like a chapter of my grieving was over. He really was still around and he was fine. I knew that. I didn't have to worry about him anymore.

I began talking a lot. I found that if you talk to people – almost everyone has at least one or two stories of communicating with those in the hereafter. I wanted to share my experiences with everyone I met, but I quickly found out that it's not always such a good idea. I had no problems talking about death. I thought it was my widow's right to talk – even joke about death. That freaks a lot of people out. But I found it hard to share how powerful these experiences were for me without making people uncomfortable, and without looking like a zealot.

What was I going to do with my life? The rest of my life? I knew what I wanted to do from pretty much the moment Truth died; I just couldn't admit it to myself. When I could admit it to myself, I still kept quiet. There's always been a big gap for me – a divide – from when I know something to when I communicate it. It's always taken me time to speak.

I continued my free style praying to God every night in front of my altar. And then I would talk to Truth. I didn't confuse the two. I knew God was not Truth and Truth was not God, but since Truth was certainly a lot closer to God than I was, I thought a three-way conversation best. The Amy who had this three-way conversation was the new Amy – the glowing Amy – the essence changed Amy with her spiritual DNA strands wrapped around a "I am good enough" mantra, a "I am perfect just the way I am" mantra. Praying calmed me and made everything seem manageable. "I don't know what I'm doing here, please guide me." This declaration from the girl who thought she knew everything.

I spent night after night praying on what I would do with my life. I had given myself a year to mourn. That seemed like a good amount of time. A year in a bubble of peace and protection, with all the time and space I needed to heal, to grow to change and then I would pop the bubble. Not in a bad way but I would venture out … where would I go?

I was raised to be very practical, especially when it comes to future and careers and money. Time should not be wasted. Money should not be wasted. One needs security. Security equals safety. Don't waste time on actions that don't lead to safety or security. Study hard, grow up, get a good paying job, buy a house, start a family, work hard, save hard, retire and then, well, die. I guess? We never got that far. It was a very traditional middle class upbringing in boxed houses with the same size boxed yard as everyone else. But my life had never followed that roadmap, and I was not about to start now, but the pressure was still there.

So when the thought crept into my head, during one of my praying sessions, that I wanted to follow the most impractical, difficult, insecure career path known to man, what was I supposed to do? Ignore it of course. I was good at that.

Really, Amy, an actor? I quickly pushed the thought to the side, hoping it would just go away. It was a ridiculous thought. I had no training. I was twenty-seven. I was still overweight by Hollywood's standards, and I was holed up in an attic in New Orleans talking to a dead man.

But, I had lost my fear. A part of me knew that wanting to be an actor was a ridiculous thought, an impractical dream. But a stronger part of me knew that thought was not true. The thought that this was ridiculous was what was ridiculous – an illusion. I could very well do anything I wanted to. Nothing was stopping me but that thought. I sat up night after night in my attic bedroom, surrounded by my photos of Truth, surrounded by my candles that were no longer burning for Truth but for me, and I plotted and planned my future. I created my future. For the first time, my future was not going to fall on top of me, happen to me, smush me – I was going to happen to it.

Of course these were just thoughts in my head. Not even spoken to the air in my attic. I wasn't quite ready to venture out into the world. I marinated in my newfound sense of joy and peace and I sopped up every last bit of it. Every last flavor seeped into my skin; I was going to need it.

I had always loved being alone, perhaps a little too much. I felt strong when I was alone. The problem was how to be myself, in the presence of others. When I was with Truth, I gave up myself. Why? I loved him was my only explanation. But why did love have to always mean I gave up me? The challenge was to share myself with other people. Not to find myself because I don't think I was ever lost. I did not feel lost now. And that's what caused the most pain. To be found, but not show it, like the girl who's been missing all these years and then comes back home but is too afraid to show herself.

On a Monday in June, I went into a session with Ben, and sat down. We exchanged pleasantries. I sat avoiding for a few minutes, scanning the room for new items on his desk, the color of his tie, admiring his curly hair; I finally nudged myself.

Looking down at the rug on the floor, I whispered, "I decided I want to be an actor."

I said it with a smile on my face because I always smiled when I was really dead serious about something – God forbid you see me powerful.

He heard me but asked anyway, "What was that?"

"I want to be an actor. I decided. That's what I want to do. Move to Los Angeles, study acting, and then I want to act."

"I'm sorry, Amy, I didn't hear you, can you say it a little louder."

"I want to be an actor." I repeated louder enunciating each syllable.

The more I said, the more force I put behind it, the stronger I became in the statement. I knew this was the life I wanted to live. I wasn't stupid or naïve. I knew the odds. I knew I was 27, ancient to get started. But I didn't care. This was the life I wanted, since I was a young girl, and I had refused to speak it. Hundreds of voices in my head telling me it was a ridiculous pipe dream. They were still in my head, but I spoke over them. You don't want to be one of those people Amy – those desperate, poor dreamers who will probably never ever succeed at it. You're not pretty enough, not skinny enough, you're too old, you're too smart for that, you'll never be able to make it. Dreams are nice but be practical. You'll never make it.

I want to be an actor. I repeated it over and over with more force. And my voice – my authentic voice became louder than all the other noise in my head. I don't know if I will fail or succeed. I don't know what will happen. Barely used to being in the driver's seat of my own life, I felt very unsteady, but I was driving.

I now had my first partner to plot with. Ben and I spent the next few weeks talking about my plans.

Twenty-seven

I had it in my head that a widow should wait at least one year before becoming intimate with another man. I have no idea where the one-year rule for widows came from, but it's out there in the universal ether. I remember a conversation I had with Truth about three months before he died. We were cooking stir-fry in the kitchen and somehow got onto the subject of what would happen if one of us died. We talked about how long we would both wait until dating someone else. I remember him giving me a hard time saying I'd probably go right out and fuck some guy within a week. Did he really think that? I got upset and said of course not. Maybe it was then when I said I'd wait at least a year. I don't remember how long he said.

So a year it was. Even though he had said to move on with my life, to not bury my head in the ground, I still thought a year was appropriate. It hadn't even crossed my mind in the first seven or eight months. But after the trip to New York, I began to feel alive again. And that went for all my bodily organs.

Nine months post Truth, I had lost seventy pounds with only fifteen left to lose. I ran and worked out three times a week with a trainer. I was getting very strong. I had never lacked sex appeal, and I knew it. It just wasn't a problem for me. And now that I had peeled off the layers of pain, I could feel my juicy self underneath.

I had never had a lot of men in my life. I took my relationships seriously, never cheated, one would end and then I would wait to start another. But after years of feeling dominated, feeling powerless, and like I was not a woman, I had some making up to do. I was soon to become the fiercely independent woman I had always wanted to be – but not quite yet. I was just venturing out of my cocoon.

In the last week of June, I met a man named Darius. He was from Los Angeles had come to New Orleans over Fourth of July for the opening of the D Day Museum, which he was involved with. A history and art buff, he also ran an Internet company. I was smitten. I told him I was a widow pretty early off; I told most everyone I met. We talked for hours each night on the phone. It felt wonderful and new to be communicating with a man, sharing my thoughts with a man who wasn't Truth. I teetered on the edge of a board, about to jump headfirst into him. He was reading a Stephen Ambrose book called D-Day. So I went out and bought it and began reading it, even though history books about wars did not interest me. But if it interested him, it would interest me. When I told him I was reading it, he was really touched and surprised that I took an interest. I liked touching him like that. I liked pleasing this stranger like that – here we go again.

He arrived to New Orleans and we made plans the first night to have dinner at Mr. B's bistro on Royal Street in the Quarter. That afternoon, in the dressing room of the Banana Republic, with the bright lights shining down on me, I turned around looking at myself in the mirror. I smiled. Not bad at all. I had on a green halter knit sweater, very pretty and feminine showing off my sculptured shoulders over a pair of khaki Capri pants that accentuated my round butt. Truth used to say no white girls he knew had my kind of butt. I must have some African in my family. I wondered what Darius would think of it.

It was July 3rd and the temperature soared as I left my townhouse. Gazing up, I saw that the sky looked like it was about to break open any minute. As the sun set, I embarked on my first date. I was beyond excited. We were meeting at the Monteleone, a luxurious and decadent hotel bar that made me feel like a girl in Paris. I let my fairy tale thoughts flow freely through my mind. I arrived ten minutes early and sat down at the bar, loving my new life. He arrived on time – with a friend.

I didn't expect someone else on our date, but was open to this adventure whatever it had in store for me. His friend was an old college buddy who lived in New Orleans and had called him last minute. Maybe this wasn't a date but I was fine with it. We all had a drink and walked across the street to the restaurant. Darius was good looking, dark hair with a strong, athletic, goes to the gym every day kind of body. He looked solid and stable – the kind of guy you could count on.

"You look beautiful. Doesn't she look beautiful?" he said to his buddy as the appetizers arrived. I smiled accepting his compliment as if I had been receiving compliments like this all my life. We talked over dinner about art and New Orleans and the food. I told them about my plans to move to Los Angeles in the new year to pursue acting. "I can see you as an actress." He said. I practiced sharing my new self. I practiced charming and glowing. Over the main course, I talked about what the last nine months had been like for me, losing my husband. I didn't go into too many details; I didn't tell him how things were actually better for me. And I didn't tell him about the visit and George. We talked about life and death but I tried to keep it light. I had two cocktails and the room with its old world New Orleans charm was looking a little hazy to me. We finished dinner and Darius asked if I wanted to go dancing after.

"Yes" the reply spilled out of my mouth even before his question ended.

He had been out all day on business and didn't have a chance to shower before dinner. He walked back to his hotel to freshen up, and we planned to meet at ten thirty on the corner of St. Ann and Bourbon to go dancing – just a few blocks from my house.

I took my time wandering back home enjoying everything about my glorious city: the air, and the heat and humidity and the people, the sound of a brass band blazing from inside a darkened club, and the smell of the French Quarter, a mixture of beer, sweat and sex. I went up to my bedroom to change. The air conditioning in the attic would not come on, and it was now close to 100 degrees. The air felt suffocating. I would never be able to sleep up there. I dragged my mattress down the stairs to my living room, so I could crash when I got home. I touched up my makeup, checked my emails, drank some water and then sat.

I waited for the minutes to tick by. I wanted to get behind them and push them along faster. I hadn't been this excited in I don't know how long. Ever? I was meeting this amazing man again. We were going dancing. He was smart and successful and good-looking, and we were going dancing. Fifteen more minutes. I switched on the TV. I switched it off. I went to the bathroom. I talked to Truth. I might kiss this man. I am moving on. And I deserve it. I deserve to be happy.

The sky opened up as I closed the door and the rain began to pour down. It rained in New Orleans in the summer like it does in the tropics: very intense, usually quite short storms that blow in and out. I had forgotten my umbrella so I ran from awning to awning. It was a Friday night and people filled the Quarter despite the weather. I arrived at the club at about 10:23 pm. There was no awning out front just a bouncer with an umbrella and a line of people. I heard the music booming from inside the courtyard.

I stood outside tall and proud and waited. I didn't want him to miss me so I stood in front and found some newspaper to cover my head from the rain. The young and old, tourists, hipsters, Goth kids, the gay crowd all mixed together in the Quarter, all with one main intention – to cut lose and have fun. Drinking on the street was legal in New Orleans and people walked by, cup in hand, downing hurricanes, daiquiris, beers, and every other liquor filled concoction you can think of. Hoots and hollers and show us your tits could be heard. In some parts of New Orleans, it seemed like Mardi Gras every day of the year. I heard zydeco music coming from a restaurant a few doors down from where I stood. The Cajun music mixed with the booming drum and bass coming from the club. Ignoring the rain, I watched the people go by and smiled. Life was going on, and I stood in the middle of it.

Five past ten thirty. My soaked newspaper began to crumble, so I threw it away. The closest awning stood two shops down and I didn't want to miss Darius so I just stood out in the rain. And I waited. And waited and waited. At ten forty-five I called his cell phone and got no answer. I checked my phone and it was fully charged with no messages. I waited some more. My hair was drenched. My chiffon turquoise top was drenched. My black

Victoria's secret camisole underneath was now drenched. And I waited. By about fifteen past eleven it dawned on me that he wasn't coming, so I stopped waiting and started walking. I walked and walked and walked until the rain stopped and the only moisture flowing was from my eyes.

Had I just been stood up? Is that what just happened? He had seemed like he was into me. He had seemed like he wanted to go out with me. He was the one who asked me to meet him. Did he just feel sorry for me? Poor Amy, the widow, we can't tell her the truth. She can't handle the truth. Had he just lied to me? Why the hell didn't he just call? I walked and felt despair and confusion.

At midnight I trudged up the stairs into my broken air conditioning, one hundred degree apartment and threw myself down on the mattress sobbing. If this was living then, fuck it, I'll go back to the walking dead life. I was in a rage. Did he not think? Did he not care? The thought that something had happened to him occurred to me, and I tried calling his cell phone two other times. Both times, I got his voicemail. I yelled some more. I had no idea how fragile I was, how easy it was to break me. Why do I put myself out there in their hands tempting them to close them around me? Enough! But I knew it was too late as I lay there trying to find all my pieces. I had done it again. I beat the mattress with my fists, kicking my feet, crying and moaning until I exhausted myself. And in the middle of my sweltering living room I fell into a deep sleep.

I am half sitting up on the mattress. It is the exact time and place as when I had fallen asleep in my French Quarter apartment. I see a small very bright orb of light that is moving in the room. I look into the light and I see what looks like an eagle flying in the light and then it turns into a tiger.

Visually I am really seeing this image in the orb. I sit up on the mattress and the right half of my body has turned prickly, kind of like what happens when you're paralyzed and can't move. The right side is where he came from. Where the light came from. Again there is an extremely bright light – small and moving but so powerful it is lighting up the whole dark room. I know it is Truth. This time I hear his voice, like an actual auditory event with my ears and at the same time I see him although it wasn't his face or form but I know it is him. First he repeats "I love you … I love you … I love you … I love you Amy" Then he calls me mon petit tete rouge. The whole auditory and visual experience lasts only 15 or 20 seconds. Then the remainder of the "dream" is me recovering from the experience. I know (still asleep) that this is not a dream that this is a real communication. And in the dream I scribble down the whole thing.

I woke up at 4:50 am Monday morning, and before I got up I wrote down the whole event word for word, as it is written here. I knew instantly as I did when I was still asleep that this was not a dream. I didn't waste any time worrying if it had really happened. I knew it was real. I knew I just had another *visit* from Truth.

I felt blessed beyond words. I felt special, so fucking special like I'm good and real and looked after. Like every desire I had had as a young girl wanting to feel safe in my skin in this world was just bestowed on me. Every cell, every molecule, every hair on my beautiful head felt right and just as it should be. Everything was just as it should be inside of me. The ramifications, like ripples flowed over my spirit, massaging away any leftover pain from the night before. The rage, the anger the confusion and despair - all gone.

I had just experienced his spirit.

Every single minute of pain he had ever caused me was forgotten. Every single *you stupid bitch*, every *you'll never amount to anything without me*, every fist meeting skin and bone, every *I'll kill you if you leave*, every chick chick of his Ruger, every single time he had ever tried to break me. Forgotten as if it was an illusion and this spirit, this light, was his true nature. He just couldn't be this when he was in his body. It didn't matter. I could not compare the weight of what I just experienced measured against the weight of the abuse. It would be an insult to what I just experienced to compare them. The pain had disappeared. The past had disappeared, and was replaced with an immeasurable amount of peace and gratefulness. It was a peace that even I could not deny. The mixed up girl in me was suffocated by the sense that this world was so much bigger and better and grander and kinder than I, in my tiny head, had ever fathomed. The grandeur and grace of what this universe really had to offer overpowered me. The lost, damaged girl of my past dissolved.

Twenty-eight

I started out counting in hours. Forty-eight, seventy-two, one hundred and twenty, and when the numbers got too high, I counted in days. Somewhere around fifty days, I started counting in weeks - eight, twelve. I counted in weeks and days for a long time. Then, I counted in months, weeks, and days. Now I was counting only in months. The exact day, the exact pin pointing of time marking the occasion of Truth's passing seemed less important to me. Did it even matter? Now it was becoming more of a measure of how long had I been living my new life.

Now everything was different. The question simply became what do I want to do. When would I leave for LA? Failure didn't frighten me in the least. I welcomed it because it meant I was testing my limits. I had attic fever.

It was at about this time, when cleaning up my computer, I came across a bookmarked website for an acting teacher in Los Angeles; I stared at the same acting studio website I had bookmarked three years ago while in fantasy mode. Back then, it was a cruel reminder of a life that I had no access to. A bookmark representing a chapter written in a language I did not understand.

Now, not only could I understand it, not only could I see it, but I was ready to touch it, ready to throw myself headfirst into it with no parachute, no net, no fear. What was the worst that could happen? I'd die?

I flew to Los Angeles the last weekend of July for a two-day private workshop with Eric Stone. We worked Saturday and Sunday from nine until five in his acting studio near Pico and Robertson. My plan was to try on acting like a pair of pants. After sixteen hours I figured I'd know if they fit or not.

I arrived fifteen minutes early on Saturday morning with a rowdy swarm of butterflies in my stomach. My body might have been fearless but my mind shook, a full on fear bunny. "I'm a kitten, you're a kitten. I'm a kitten, you're a kitten." I had heard that somewhere and it calmed me to chant it.

I felt like I had walked into a force of nature upon first entering into his studio and meeting Eric. His power reminded me of Truth, except he was more of a tidal wave, while Truth had been a tornado. As soon as I stepped into his studio I experienced the energy, and if I let myself, I knew I would get completely swept up into it. To say Eric was passionate about life and art and acting was the understatement of the century. French, in his mid-forties, very good looking with thick curly brown hair, hazel eyes, he oozed charm in the way French men can without even trying.

I was very honest with Eric that I did not have a lot of experience or training in acting. I had done bits and pieces here and there in high school and college but had never allowed myself to take it seriously.

"Are you open?" he asked.

"Yes."

"Do you trust me?"

"Well, I just met you."

"That's not what I asked. Do you trust me?"

"Sure. Yes. I trust you." And I meant that.

"Then you'll do just fine," he said with a smile.

He had dedicated his life for the last twenty-five years to acting, teaching and now painting. He left France at eighteen for New York with no money but lots of dreams. He studied with some of the great teachers in New York: Uta Hagen, Herbert Berghof and Stella Adler. He was an honorary member of the Actor's Studio; he performed on Broadway and in the soaps for many years. He had been in Los Angeles for the past twelve years, acting and teaching.

The studio was two rooms at the end of a hallway that ran between a Thai restaurant and a tailor. There was a small office and the second room was a roughly four hundred square foot open space – half taken up by a raised stage with black walls, black ceiling and black floors and the other half of the room was carpeted with cushiony bench seating around the three wood paneled walls. It was nothing special as far as aesthetics, but it was quiet and in the evenings and weekends, actors could make as much noise as they needed.

On Saturday morning, Eric began giving me background on the work of the actor. "Actors are like athletes of the heart," he said. I liked that.

"I don't know where to start," I commented nervously as he had me sit up on stage by myself.

"Start from where you are right now. You. Amy. What's going on with you right now."

"I'm scared shitless."

"Then be scared shitless."

"Yeah. That's what I'm doing."

"No, you're thinking about being scared shitless, and you're thinking about how you look. Don't think. Acting is not intellectual, I hate to break that news to you. Acting is about doing."

"I don't know what I should be doing."

"Do whatever you want to do as long as you're in the being."

"What?"

"And then when you're not being scared shitless anymore, than be what you ever comes up for you next."

"What do you mean *be*?"

"Be. Just be. Don't try to hide it. Don't think about it. Don't talk about it. Just sit in it. Be."

"Oh of course, be." Silly me.

That was the gist of the first day: Eric saying something that seemed logically very easy and me getting completely confused and lost.

We did some exercises designed to bring up emotions. I stood awkwardly on the stage repeating Get Away, pushing my arms outwards from me. I had to do it with full commitment like I really meant it and express whatever came up. It was not easy at all for me. Seemingly simple but thoughts and images from my childhood would come up and I would stuff them back down.

"You have a lot of anger. Are you aware of that?"

I giggled.

"Why are you laughing?"

I giggled again unable to stop myself. "I'm sorry."

"What are you sorry for?"

"I don't know." I wasn't used to people talking to me the way Eric did. I wasn't used to having every action I made, everything I said being watched, and I wasn't used to being held accountable for it.

"Tell me, does your anger have permission to come out? What are you not allowed to do up on that stage? What are you not allowed to feel?"

"I don't know." I was feeling overwhelmed and my head started going foggy. "A lot, I guess."

My homework that night was to come up with six to eight characters that I had inside of me – whether they had permission to come out or not – and do an improvised demonstration of them on Sunday. How would they stand, how would they walk, cross their legs, talk, what would they do? I went back to the hotel exhausted but elated. I had no idea what I was doing and it felt good, not knowing, not caring, and doing it anyway. I was attracted to Eric and loved the energy I felt when I was around him. It was powerful energy, scary but also gentle. I ordered a hamburger from room service and got to work exploring who was inside of me. What characters wanted to come out to play? It was fun, like a game. I came up with the following: the crazy girl (emotionally unstable), the seductress girl (she had been dormant for many years but was still there), the obedient girl (the yes girl), the victim girl (abused wife), the grieving girl (widow), the opinionated, angry bitch (not a girl) and the athlete. I practiced them in my hotel room even though Eric said not to practice; just get in touch with and explore he said. The demonstrations were to be spontaneous.

The next day we started with my characters. I let myself go, something I had never done before. I didn't care how I looked or if it would be good. I jumped into the characters not even remembering what I did afterwards. The seductress, angry bitch and athlete were the most seamless he said. I was the most in the being. The others were interpretations of what I thought it should look like and therefore came out clichéd.

"The others were not really you. Maybe they were who you thought you were but they were not authentic. You must approach every character from the point of view of who YOU really are."

"But I am a widow. I have been grieving. I was an abused wife." I had given Eric some of my background when we talked by email, so this wasn't news to him.

"Oh really, so that's who you really are. If I look you up in the dictionary in the stars that's what it will say under Amy Lewis: widow, abused wife. How sad."

"NO!" His comment pissed me off. "No ... but I have been that, so it's still inside of me."

"But is it who you really are?"

"NO. No." I said like the obstinate child ... "I don't know who I *really* am."

Eric jumped from his seat and bellowed "Ah Hahhh" with such volume and fierceness that I almost fell out of my chair. "Maybe that's why you're here."

"Maybe it is," I said with a confused smile.

By Sunday evening I was completely exhausted, mostly confused but quite sure of one thing: the pants fit. I was keenly aware of how late in life I was starting and how long it takes to develop as an actor. Ten years, Eric said, it can take ten years for an actor to develop properly. It doesn't happen overnight. Fine, I don't care, I said. We made plans. I would return in a few months to look for a place to live, and we'd have another session. Then when

I arrived in January we would work together privately and I would then join his studio classes.

The energy flowing through the space was amazing; it was all about possibility. The opposite of what I was used to in my internal world. The energy said anything is possible. It's all within reach. Invigorated, happy, turned on and very awake, we talked. Eric told me about his painting; he was producing volumes of work the past few years. He had a stack of photos of his work – pastels, oils and mixed media paintings. Much of his art was highly abstract and expressionistic with bold, inviting colors with big brush strokes. I liked what I saw. I flipped through the photos in my hand. One after another until I got to almost the bottom of the pile when I saw them – two photos of two of his paintings. The first a tiger staring straight at me and the next an eagle flying with wings swept out. I placed them next to each other on the stage floor and inspected them closely my mouth open.

"Oh God." I looked over at him sitting six feet across from me. I knew these images. I had seen them less than a month ago. "Oh shit" I mumbled. My eyes welling up. "When did you paint these?" I said it more forcefully than I had intended.

"Those? Sometime last year. Why? What's the matter?"

This couldn't be. This was so weird. They were the same images. The same. Weird. Weird. Coincidence? This has got to be a coincidence. Things like this just don't happen. Oh fuck. Am I making this all up? I scrutinized them closer bringing them up to the light from the halogen lamp sitting next to me. No. I knew better. The last year of my life had taught me that. This was not a coincidence.

"Hello? Earth to Amy … remember me? Come back to the studio. What's wrong?"

I looked up at him and then back down at the pictures of the tiger and eagle. "How much time do you have?"

"A lot. So spit it out."

So I spit. I told him about the visit. About the first one with the touch and electricity and then the session with George and then about the second one with the orb of light that lit up my whole room and his voice and the images of the tiger and eagle. He was open. He was visibly moved by the story I was telling him. He believed me!

"I don't know what this means Eric … but it feels good. It feels right. I feel amazing. I think I've found my teacher."

We said our goodbyes and I flew back to New Orleans. On the flight back home, I settled into my seat next to the window looking out at the big puffy cumulus clouds, and I sank into the calm spread over my body. If I died right now, I'd be happy. It was the first time I could say that. I felt right inside. I had lined myself up with time, right on top of it and my right hand was aligned perfectly with where my right hand was exactly where it wanted to be … my left ear lobe was right up there where it wanted to be, my tongue was in place, my pinkie was in place, and god knows my pussy was in the right place, and it felt so good to be just where I felt I was supposed to be. There was no I wish I could, there was no I wish I had, there was no if only, there was no but I can't – just I am … I am doing exactly what I want to be doing.

I had four months to prepare myself for Los Angeles. I moved through the days with a calm sense of purpose and grace. Grace was not a word I had ever used in conjunction with myself. But everything was changing now after the session with George, the last visit from Truth and meeting Eric. All these experiences had brought me into a new sense of peace that I could not deny, nor could I mess with. I was different, and I knew it. I felt for once that I was on a path. Actually walking on a path instead of lying in a ditch next to one.

Weeks before I had ordered a personalized license plate with TRUTH on it. When it arrived, I immediately walked down the block on Dauphine to where my Miata was parked with screwdriver in hand. An old Italian man standing out front of the corner grocery store smiled at me as I stood up after attaching the new plate to the back of my car. "Ahh the Truth" he said with his heavy Italian accent "Truth shall set you free, yes Bella?"

"Yes." I smiled back at him. "Yes he shall."

I picked up the GAMBIT as I walked back to my townhouse. I flipped through the weekly paper, a combination of local news, entertainment and classifieds. I perused the personals in the back section. Curious and lonely, I had taken to reading them. I wanted to sleep with a man – ninety percent out of loneliness and ten percent wanting to get it over with. There was still a miniscule part of me that feared Truth would come down from the heavens and show up at my front door looking to beat up the man who I chose to share my bed. I knew from the sting of my first date fiasco weeks ago that I was not looking for a boyfriend. I wasn't even looking for a second date. I wanted one night with a stranger.

I don't remember what I said when I left this man a voicemail message. I cannot even remember his name, so I'll call him Adam. He was younger than me by a few years and new to New Orleans. He came from some small Southern town to New Orleans for its art scene. He was a musician and artist and Caucasian. We met at the Tricou House, a bar and club that had funky sexy cabaret shows on the weekends but it was a weeknight so there were no shows, just a half empty bar with Blue neon lights along the top.

As we sat at the bar and got very tipsy on martinis, I told him about myself and my life and my situation. I told him I hadn't been with a man since it happened. I told him I felt ready. And I told him I wanted him to be that man. He felt very innocent and this is why I chose him. Not a rough bone on his body. He was taken aback by my directness and my lack of wasted time.

"So what do you think?" I asked as I was finishing my second apple martini. I could not deal with another rejection, and I didn't want to beg.

"Are you sure this is what you want to do?" he asked me.

I nodded my head, sipping the last drop from my glass.

"I am attracted to you but maybe we should take this slower."

"Slow is good, but as long as slow starts and ends tonight. I'm not looking for more than that."

I don't think he knew what to make of me. Perhaps I was being unfair, a bit manipulative. I wanted to offer only what I wanted and nothing more. One night was all that was on the table. I was relieved when he took my hand giving it a tight squeeze and grabbed the check.

"Then we should go."

He walked me up to my place holding my hand, soft and gentle and easy and warm and I led him up into my private attic bedroom and into my bed. It was dark and we slowly undressed each other. For hours we simply ran our fingers over each other's body — slow and light as a feather barely caressing the skin. He touched me with his flesh filled with compassion and tame, sweet gentleness. For hours we sat upwards with legs wrapped around each other and stared into each others eyes with just the moonlight from the window and two candles on my alter next to Truth's picture bringing light to the room. Delicate tears grew around my eyes and he would wipe them away with the tips of his fingers and then his kisses. It was the most honest lovemaking I had ever known. I had never felt that present before with a man.

The next morning he did not want to leave, but I stuck to my game plan. One night was all I could handle. I suggested breakfast at Croissant D'Or. We sat in the corner by the window in a tiny café table for two. I spoke quietly as I buttered my croissant.

"You have no idea how good last night felt to me. You gave me exactly what I needed." I put my hand on his as he sipped his coffee.

"I know you probably won't use it, but here's my number." He scribbled it on the napkin.

I looked down as I took the napkin, knowing he was right, I would not use it. A few hours of honesty and gentleness was all I could handle. It was like I had a time limit to allow goodness into me and once I was filled up, I could not let more in. There was too much room inside me still taken up by demons.

"Thank you." We hugged and this nameless Adam man who now in my recollection seems more like a boy got into his car and drove away. I threw his number into a garbage can and quietly walked home enjoying the bright morning rays and the feeling of fresh sex in between my legs.

Twenty-nine

On the third of January 2001, once again I packed up a U-Haul, and my Dad drove with me out west – to Los Angeles. I insisted that I could drive out by myself. I was drunk with my independence and power. His response was something to the effect of "Over my dead body."

We crossed the country again, my dad and I. My parents were used to my crisscrossing the county and to saying goodbye. I didn't know a soul in California other than my teacher. "Sure I know people out there." I told them so they wouldn't worry. My fear slowly began to creep back. It had only been thirteen months since Truth died; sometimes it still seemed like yesterday. And I was in a huge, strange city completely on my own. Deep Breathes Amy. I remembered walking in to the ICU room to see Truth's dead body – if I could do that, I could do anything.

I found a small apartment in Topanga. I made a deliberate decision to keep myself protected and separate from Hollywood and "the business" for as long as I needed to settle into my life in LA and into the craft of acting. Topanga, being a rural mountain community, was the perfect spot for this. Even though I was just twenty minutes from LA, I felt like I was in another world, of peace, serenity and natural beauty. I would not take the typical route of many actors fresh off the bus and let myself get caught up in the craziness and headiness of being an actor in LA. I would not get headshots, would not try to get an agent, and would not go on any auditions – not until I was ready. The apartment that I rented was the bottom floor of a house owned by a playwright and his wife. They were very kind and took care of me, being a single woman new to town. I impressed myself that I didn't tell them I was a widow. I considered it a great leap that I did not play the W card.

My redheaded porn site supported me, giving me the luxury to dedicate myself fully to acting. Despite still feeling deeply conflicted about the porn industry, I channeled my love and energy into the site. I created one final alias, Nina Rouge, who ran All Redheads using my face. Nina was in honor of my favorite blues singer, Nina Simone. I was owner and producer of the site, not a model. But the women I hired were like extensions of me, and I portrayed them as powerful, erotic Goddesses. I branded the site as an exclusive club for distinguished gentlemen who preferred real redheads. The Playboy Channel did a story on the site; for the segment, I gathered ten natural redheads for a playful, artsy shoot in the green mountains of Topanga. I might still be a pornographer (I didn't kid myself), but I was a high-end pornographer.

I felt like the site allowed me to express my sensuality, be creative and make a good living, but the downside was the guilt that I could not let go of. I realize it was the shame of someone else's imposed morality that I had taken on. Inside, I wasn't ashamed of my sexuality. It was showing how powerful I am, my sensual, emotional, and creative power – the power of being a woman. I was ashamed of that.

My side project was launching a site that explored beauty and brains; I was trying to find and convince beautiful, exceedingly intelligent women to pose nude. The site had a catch – men would only get to see their photos after reading whatever scholarly article, research or report they had most recently written. I admit recruitment was no going so well.

Eric came to my place for the weekly sessions. I attended classes at the studio on Wednesdays and Sundays. We videotaped all of our private sessions, over two hundred hours. The plan was simple: my desire was to be a working actress. Anything that got in the way of that – we would open up, look at and overcome. Consciously, we created a space where everything and anything was ok to come out – as long as it forwarded our intention. Our sessions were a little unusual – a little out of the ordinary for acting training; I was like an egg and inside was an artist, but before she could hatch, we had to shine a very bright light on her to keep her warm, to give her time to grow – these were my incubation sessions.

I had an assignment to explore who I would be without my "drama" and express it in performance. We had been talking about the good girl inside of me that suppressed all of the feelings and thoughts I did not allow myself. During the week, I was inspired to make a life size cardboard cut-out of this good girl, from the leftover Ikea box of my bookshelves. On her body I wrote all the things she told me when she was suppressing me: "you're not good enough", "Victim", "Scardy Cat", "You're ugly, fat", "Don't speak too loud", "Don't make a scene". Then I hung her from a rope from my curtain rod. Needless to say I lived alone, and had yet to bring the new friends I was meeting to my apartment. So no one knew I lynched my suppressor except Eric.

To express my new no drama self, I bought a sparkly, fire-engine red, tight-fitting dress and a CD of Shania Twain's "Feel like a Woman". I performed a sexy, strutty modern dance routine – expressing who I would be without my drama. He was impressed and was easily convinced that I completed the assignment. I changed clothes and we continued the session.

"Let's do some relaxation work and see what shows up."

I hated relaxation work. No relaxation for Amy. The exercises had become my nemesis. It was simple. Repeat long, loud solid sounds of Maaaa and channel whatever emotions you are feeling through the sound. Always hard for me.

I began as I always did, feeling like an idiot, "maaaaaaaaaaaaaaaaa," smiling at first as I made the noise. Then my smiles and giggles melted into frustration and the frustration melted into a hint of anger but quickly changed back to frustration and then I shut down and felt nothing repeating in robotic, monotone "maaaaaaa". I stopped the exercise myself, thoroughly blocked.

After I opened up my eyes, Eric said, "My question to you is this: When it comes to anger, why is it not okay for you to express it?"

"You noticed it's the one thing I didn't write up on my suppressor – no accident there."

"You sit on a lot of stuff Amy. We don't need to analyze it. As artists, we don't need to know what it is or where it comes from or why it's there. What we need to know is that all these feelings have a certain energy to them that needs to be gathered and gotten in touch with so that it can be released. What's not cool is that you have all this energy but you spend more time trying to pretend it's not there, more time avoiding, questioning what the hell it is, rather than just gathering it up and vroom out.

You have some interpretation about your anger – a point of view about it – that you are unwilling to share. And as an artist, to not share is not cool."

How dare he call me a non-sharing person? I was very generous. But he kept going on and on, and my head felt cloudy.

"You might have the impulse to kill. But you reinterpret it at a higher level, and you make it into something beautiful and artistic."

I don't want to kill anyone. Shut up, I wanted to say. Just stop talking. But he didn't.

"You have no permission to express your stuff. You give yourself permission to feel it – you feel it all over the place – but you don't communicate it – you don't express it. So the feelings just stay exactly where they are. What you're sitting on is the actual angle – the point of view about your anger – it could be something like this – I have a right to be mad you asshole. It's my fucking business if I want to be mad. This is an opportunity for you Amy – use your stuff. You've got a lot of it."

Why is he going on? Can't he just leave me alone? Finally I got the nerve to speak and I lashed out.

"I'm sick of hearing you tell me what a wonderful opportunity this is. Don't tell me when to express my anger and when not to express it."

"Who's telling you that? When did I say that?"

"Ok, you didn't say that. To you this is all just a game, and I have twenty-five more minutes in this session and then I have to go back to work, and I have to do things to make a living, and if I have all this anger going through my head, I can't do this. And you go home, and you don't have all this anger. And you just think this is all fun and this is acting and this is art – this isn't art to me."

"Amy, don't make this about me. Those feelings are there anyway. You have just cleverly found ways to hide them from yourself. And since you're smart, you hide them from others too. But if you don't get in touch with them, see what's there, and begin to let them out, they're going to kill you. Acting or no acting. Don't make this about the exercise and don't make it about me."

"I'm confused. My head is swirling and I don't know what I'm supposed to feel."

"Tell the truth. Something you haven't thought about. Tell the truth. The truth."

"The truth about what?"

"The truth about how you feel. You're fighting with your truth and the only thing is I have you locked up here for two hours with all the back doors locked so you have no way to get out of this. All I'm interested in is the truth."

"Sometimes I hate that word."

"You play a lot of games Amy. I don't mean you but your ego plays a lot of games with you."

"I don't know what the simple truth is."

"It doesn't start with 'I don't know' or 'I'm confused'. You sit on a lot of anger Amy. You think it's any coincidence that you attracted Truth into your life? You think you two were all that different? Only difference is he expressed his rage. You kept yours locked inside. Now, tell me the truth about how you feel right now. Just be real. Trust yourself is all I'm asking. You're doing much better than you realize but you have all these ways of avoiding yourself."

"I feel put on the spot here, I feel like I have to go to the bathroom but don't want to again, I feel like fuck I wanted this to be a good session but it doesn't seem like it is now."

I looked at him and wanted to run. I wanted to shut down to go unconscious to do anything but listen to him say these things. I knew this feeling very well. I could feel the rage bubbling under the surface. I knew he was right. And I also knew I wanted to be here.

"Amy put your hand your heart and just tell me what's there." He was getting exasperated with me.

Fine. Fine. FINE! I put my hand on my heart and closed my eyes and began hearing the words: I don't need anyone, I don't need anyone, I don't need anyone's help. Then quick as a flash, Truth's burial scene came before my eyes. I see bright sunlight, everybody outside at the cemetery on the hillside just off the 80 freeway – his family, my family walking to the plot. My mom approaches me from behind and reaches out taking my hand in hers. She wanted to tell me something, to explain something.

"I thought you needed your space. That's why I didn't sit next to you."

My space? Hours earlier in the church, I had sat with Barbara, Tessa and Allison and Truth's aunties and grandmother; my mom, dad and sister sitting a few rows back. My space? My space? On that day … that day of all days … the day I buried my husband you thought I needed my space? I needed you. I needed you around me, holding me, comforting me. I needed *you*, mom.

The memory vanished and deep sobs overtook my body. He left me alone until I came out of it. I opened my eyes feeling tired but also lighter, clearer. And the anger was gone.

"Now you know. Now you know – for today – that was what you were sitting on. And now it's out of you. Tomorrow it will probably be something different."

"I never told her that Eric. I didn't want to hurt her feelings."

"Well this is what happens to the nice girl act. The nice girl actually hides a lot of anger – a lot of rage."

"I'm sick of hurting myself with this stuff, Eric."

"You don't have to. As an actress, you're creating a container that says I have a right to my feelings and my point of view about my feelings – but I don't have to make it mean anything past the expression of it. It doesn't mean ANYTHING that you're mad at your mother about this. In your personal life, yes maybe it means something to you – that's none of my business. But using it on stage – there is no meaning attached to it, no repercussions, no guilt. The paradox is you have to express it fully. You can't do it half-assed. You have to do it as if you were going to kill your mom. Half ass – go to therapy. Don't do it in acting – it's too noble of an art. In life, you don't get to do things for real. The irony of the stage is that it feels real to the actor, to the audience, it looks real, you get the release from doing it as if it was real but NONE of it is real, and it means absolutely nothing. Let me say that again, it means absolutely nothing. And in meaning nothing – it can mean everything."

Our sessions were intense. I finished them exhausted or elated or some combination of the two. Much of our work, in the first six months, was about me getting over my resistance. "You're hard headed," Eric had told me many times, so it was taking longer to do this work. But when we did get underneath, I discovered what I had inside of me that I could bring out and play with on stage. I switched back and forth between raw when I was in the thick of my stuff and positively beaming with energy and joy when I had freed myself from it. When beaming, I attracted people right and left to me. Making friends and attracting people was as easy as opening my mouth and talking. I had never experienced such power and freedom.

I was peeling off my layers, and just when I thought I had reached some plateau of nirvana, I would find another raw spot that sent me barreling towards another dark hole. It was in one of these very dark holes I was sitting in when he arrived to my place one afternoon in March.

I had gone on a mind trip that day. I do not remember the nature of what sent me there. My trips seemed to be very long and very far away, and I never told anyone where I went. I would just be missing, unconscious, for a period of time and then I'd come back. I had become brilliant at disguising these trips. When you live alone, it's very easy to do this. I have probably spent four to five years of my life missing, if you added up all the trips, back to back. But here Eric was on my front doorstep, and since I had asked him to coach me and since I knew he wouldn't come to where I was – he flat out refused to teach me when I went "on a trip" – I knew I'd have to come back in a little. So I crawled three quarters of the way back, enough so we could talk.

"I'm getting to the end of my rope." I had no emotional affect and stared out the window of my living room into the Topanga forest. "Something still has a hold of me and won't let go. I'm having panic attacks. I feel like I can't breathe, like there's not enough oxygen in the room. I can't take being alone anymore. I miss Truth."

"Sometimes when we get to these difficult places where we don't know what's up and what's down, it helps to go back to the basics. Like what do you want?"

"I want to not feel like this. Shitty. Depressed. Hopeless. That's what I want. Resigned like what the fuck am I doing here, wanting to be an actor? I'm not an actor. I'm not an artist. I thought I was through with all this shit, and here I am again. I can't sleep, I can't think, I can't work, and, God knows, I can't create anything. All I can create is this – here's my self-portrait." I drew a black blob with a felt tip marker.

"You've got to stop attacking yourself. Give yourself a break. The lack of peace and joy in your life is now becoming evident and is now intolerable to you. You've seen that you can choose differently. But now you've come to a standstill realizing that you really have the power to choose."

"That's how I feel when I'm having the panic attacks like I can't move, can't live this way anymore."

"You have to make the transition a peaceful one, a gentle one. The war is over, Amy. You need to call a truce and start declaring peace."

My head spun. I had a hard time following his words. He just kept talking and talking and talking about war and peace, and I stared at his lips moving so fast and I had a difficult time connecting his words to me.

"What is your big judgment about gentleness? To be gentle simply means you're incapable of attack. It is the total opposite of attack thoughts. You need to get more vigilant about your attack thoughts. In your case you use your intelligence to mask your desire to war."

"What are you talking about?"

"You're a warrior, Amy. You love to fight. You always have. You're either the one doing the attacking on yourself or you're allowing others to attack you when you switch to the victim role – another way to attack yourself. Is there any part of you that genuinely wants out of this? You talk a good talk Amy – you fool a lot of people – but I say what's inauthentic about you – what's full of shit about you is that you want to stop warring. You don't. You love it too much. Now if you could honestly admit that. We'd start moving a lot faster."

"Eric, I thought you were supposed to be helping here, not making me feel worse."

"I am not here to make you feel better, goddammit! You should go get a fucking therapist if that's what you want. I don't care how you feel. You're feelings are not really you anyway. What I want, what you hired me to do is to free you up from your personal, boring bullshit so you can create some space – some freedom to create from. As an artist."

"That sounds great. Wonderful! But these are just words to me. All I know… All I care about right now is that this shit, my personal, BORING bullshit is KILLING me."

"I'm saying you're full of shit! And only one of us is right. And if I'm right then what is this all about? You've been on this mean, vengeful path, killing everything in sight."

I'm in tears now feeling completely misunderstood.

"Eric, I'm serious. This is killing me."

"No – it – is – not!"

"You don't know what I feel." Sobbing now.

"Only one of us is right, Amy. You choose. Go ahead, choose. Either it's killing you or it's not. Are you dying right now? Should I call the paramedics?"

"Fine, it's not killing me."

"Then what is all this about? What is all this you're doing, sweetie?"

I sat quietly, and stopped the crying. It was very easy to turn off the tears. I went inside my head and it wasn't cloudy anymore. I looked up at him. I was fully present for the first time in days. Back from my trip.

"I know. I know you're right. I hate admitting it."

"More attack."

"I know. I should just stay quiet."

"Yes do that. In fact close your eyes and imagine you're a brilliant warrior, the best all over the land. You've been fighting your entire life and you're in the middle of a giant battlefield, red hair flowing in the wind, killing right and left, destroying everything you see, blood squirting in all direction, limbs flying. You're holding a giant sword three times the length of your arm and mid swing, you suddenly freeze. All the action stops, and you realize for the first time in your life, you gasp as you realize you've been on a war path. Your whole life has been about destroying, but you didn't realize it because you were too busy doing it."

"I'm there."

"Now, forgive yourself for that. You are where you are, Amy. Let yourself be there."

"I don't want to be where I'm at."

"That's how you get yourself into trouble. If you like to destroy then admit it, and use it. Throw it all into your work – become the baddest, meanest, most intense bad girl you can be if that's where you're at right now. It's an amazing opportunity. But my coaching to you is in your personal life – drop the warring. I've never met anyone with as much strength and resilience as you Amy … but you need to temper it with gentleness. You need to give yourself a break."

Even the hardest of heads has a soft spot. And slowly, Eric's words found their way in through my soft spot. I let him in and I had fewer and fewer of those bad days. When I did go "on trips" I was able to come back quickly. I found myself with a lot of space around me, space that used to be filled with my boring personal bullshit. Now I could fill that space with … well, with whatever I wanted.

Thirty

A few weeks after this session, I sat down at my desk and vomited. When I looked down five minutes later I saw that I had vomited out a poem – that's how it came out, violent, spewing, chunky, and fast. So fast that I needed to make sure the paper was long and wide or the words would spill out over my desk and get lost on the floor. But when it was all out, I felt better. Lighter. And the pain in my stomach, the anxiety in my chest had disappeared. I could breathe again.

I was exuberant. I had written a poem. Now I wanted to share it. I googled poetry readings in Los Angeles. I was not one to write for five years before getting up the nerve to read it in public. I wanted to go public now. The next reading was Friday at 8 pm at Midnight Special on 3rd Street Promenade in Santa Monica. I had two hours to eat and get myself there.

Midnight Special was an independent bookstore, one of the few fighting to stay alive in the world of big corporate booksellers. It reminded me of Cody's bookstore on Telegraph in Berkeley – lots of revolutionary, activist vibes. They held the reading in a room in the back of the bookstore surrounded by books on all sides and open on one side so that customers could stand in the back and listen. It was the longest running open mic poetry reading in Los Angeles; it had been going on for over twenty years. Almost every poet in Los Angeles had read there at one time.

The host was a balding, sensual man named Reverend Dan – a Reverend of the word. I signed my name on the list and sat in the back row, my stomach gnawing with nervous energy. The thirty or so chairs filled up fast and Reverend Dan began calling the poets up randomly from the list. It was a hodgepodge mix of literary poets, some of which bored me, comics who were practicing new material which no one seemed to mind that they weren't really poems and energetic spoken word poets spewing out their rage and pain and hope. The guy two rows ahead of me kept turning out checking me out. He looked like that actor who was accused of killing his wife. I smiled back at him my sweet and innocent I'm just a girl smile – this was my smile for when I was nervous. Reverend Dan called my name, and I let go of nervousness and glided up to the podium.

"Hi everyone. My name's Amy."

"Hi. .. hello … Hi Amy … Hey"

I felt like I was in an AA meeting. "Ummm .. so this is my first time reading … my first time writing too." I got lots of clapping and encouragement. Always good to keep their expectations low.

"Ok … here goes it's called Waking up in the Gap. … but not the clothing store." I got some laughs. I tapped the microphone and opened my mouth …

What do you do when everything you've ever done,
Doesn't do it for you anymore?

What do you do,
When your illusions are gone,

When your delusions are gone,
When your delusionary illusions are gone,
When they don't fucking work anymore.
What do you do to fill up that space?
What do you do when you need to fixate?
So you try inebriation … but it doesn't work.
So you try casual sexation … but it doesn't work.
You're getting desperate … and desperate … and desperate,
The hole inside is screaming for a fix …What do you do?

What do you do when everything you've ever done,
Doesn't do it for you anymore?

Give me a man damnit!
Get me a cock!
Give me a drink dammit!
Get me a shot!
Get me a late-night pig out of every
Morsel in sight!
Get me a Vegas spree,
A spending spree …
A destructive spree … a spree a spree,
A spree … a noisy frolic … a period of
Uninhibited activity … that's what I want.
That's what I need … that's what I crave …
I try and I try and I try but it doesn't work anymore.

What do you do when everything you've ever done,
Doesn't do it for you anymore?

What Freedom Smells Like

I need to DOOOOOO something,
Something has to be done,
To fill it up,
To patch it up to eat it up to sew it up to fix it up.

I want the days when I can fantasize freely,
When I could fuck freely,
When I could destruct freely,
When I could war freely,
When I could hurt freely,
I want those days back.

I don't care that they are illusions.
They served me well. They kept me
Satisfied, satiated, medicated, intoxicated,
Fixated, hydrated.

What do you do when everything you've ever done,
Doesn't do it for you anymore?

What do you do,
When you stand in front of your mirror, naked,
Looking at yourself,
QUIET and CALM,
Seeing *you* for the first time.
Seeing that you need nothing,
want nothing, lack for nothing
That you do not already have.

What do you do when everything you've ever done,
Doesn't do it for you anymore?

You take a deep breath.
And you do NOTHING.

I closed my mouth and stood back from the microphone. It was very quiet. I had performed with every ounce of passion in my body, a considerable amount. I looked out and everyone began to clap. Not 'the oh isn't that nice clapping' or the 'let's be polite' kind, but the distinctive, loud, rousing 'we really get you' kind of clapping. The 'wow we didn't expect that' kind of clapping.

Later, I was invited to the poets' after party. I didn't even know poets had after parties. It was at Dan's apartment on the beach in Venice. I walked home late that night quenched. It was astonishing to me that I could be in a state of emotional pain and desperation at 5pm, depressed, lost and regressing and then vomit out the emotions in a daisy chain of words on paper and then go to a place where I had never been, and didn't know anyone and then share my daisy chain of words which didn't look like vomit anymore and get real applause and have people come up to me after and tell me that they appreciated my words that could have been cuts long ago and then party with them and feel not one iota of the pain I had just felt 7 hours before. Feel alive and awake and conscious and loved and connected. Simply astonishing to me. I was a woman who had been dehydrated all my life but didn't understand the nature of my ailment until I tasted my first glass of water. They got me. And I got me. I got that I needed to be gotten. I skipped back to my car and went home to find another pocket of me that needed getting.

"I felt at home in my skin Eric. I'd never felt that at home. That right with things." I was telling him about the poetry reading. "I have spent so much time in my life thinking I didn't have anything worth sharing in a creative realm … and now that I'm out of that – free from that – I see other people sharing, and I say I want to do that."

"And you are."

"I am."

"You've been able to make a distinction – to see a distinction between your pain, which is all your judgment focused mind, and the truth. That's no small feat. Now, Art will be you teacher, but you're not quite in touch with the artist in you."

"I think I am."

"You're getting there but you haven't made a choice yet. If you're an artist or a bourgeois consumer."

"How do I do this?"

"It's easy. You keep writing every day. And you find out what all the teaching is about. Art becomes your teacher when you let it teach you about your path. You are discovering your path Amy. It's not hard to tune in to it, what's hard is to keep walking it. Your program, your plan is just that: walk it. Just write. Write with everything you are, everything you feel, what you are and what you aren't. Just keep walking your moment."

"You know I thought I came out here to be an actor – I wanted to be famous, my picture in magazines, and I still want to act but not for those reasons. I just want to be an artist – to express myself however I want to be expressed. I'm a happy girl Eric."

"You don't have to tell me that. It's emanating from every pore in your body."

For three years and over a hundred and fifty sessions, Eric continued to push me into the world of my imagination and timelessness. It was in this place that I found myself. That I found my voice, my drive, my fire, and I found myself finally standing right in front of the glowing beautiful woman that I had always known was there. And there she was just waiting for me to wake up and see her.

I had survived the event that psychologists say is one of the worst a person has to go through. I truly got that life is eternal and I got the astounding sense of peace that came with it, and I knew exactly what I wanted to dedicate my life to. That is power. I would drive around Los Angeles amazed, so happy to be living this life, so happy to be one of the hundred thousand or so struggling actors in Los Angeles. I walked through the Paramount lot one night getting off of a background gig on *Nip/Tuck* and I couldn't stop laughing as I walked. That I was another head in the clouds, unknown actor cliché didn't bother me at all. I loved it. I was doing exactly what I wanted.

My dark side never went away, but I had found a way to use it. Every single one of my demons, from the crazy girl, to the depressed girl, to the slut girl, to the battered wife, to the rageful girl could be channeled into a character. Or they could be chan-neled into a story or poem as I began to write and discover I could find myself there as well. That I could be lost in a black hole somewhere and write myself out of it.

Gradually, I stopped counting time. I lost track of how long it had been since Truth died. I lost track of all the anniversaries and special dates we shared, except October 11th, which I decided to celebrate as my second birthday. My rebirthday. I have never gone to his grave since the funeral, and refuse as I know he's not there.

Thirty-one

The years flew by and I continued acting, writing, creating and performing. My connection to the woman I had been with Truth had all but disappeared. The one thread that remained was the malpractice lawsuit. The review board decided in my favor, paving the way for what could have been a successful malpractice lawsuit. I met the doctor face-to-face at the review board hearing – the one who came in that first night and did nothing. I had imagined him a monster in my memory, but he didn't appear that way in court. He approached me looking kinder and gentler, and he shook my hand contritely. I knew that continuing on with the lawsuit would not bring me any solace. I had found my answers another way, so I settled the case, splitting, about sixty thousand dollars after the attorney's cut, with Truth's daughters. I think my attorneys were not pleased that I settled for such a small amount, when we could have gotten much more had we gone to trial. But I didn't want to play the part of a grieving widow anymore.

I felt expressed, content and as though I were moving forward, but also very lonely. I wondered if I could call a man into my life. I felt ready. Four years since Truth had died and I had gotten him out of my system. I had dated a lot of different men and I knew more about what I liked and didn't like. I was clear that I didn't love any of these men I dated, and also clear that I would know it when the right man came along. I was ready to be a part of a relationship. But this time, it would be so different. I would not lose myself. I would be healthy and be myself and be with a man at the same time – a novel concept. I decided to summon up all my female powers to call him. I would put it out to the universe that I was ready. I would surround myself with pinkness – turn my bedroom into a giant wet and ready vagina.

"Can you tell me where vagina pink is?" I asked the salesmen in Home Depot paint department. Ok. I didn't really ask him that. But I did explain to him my plan minus the vagina.

Two weeks after the paint dried, I met a man from Africa. I remember on our first date writing his 5-syllable name out phonetically on the dinner napkin to make sure I could pronounce it and I kept repeating it over and over the next day. His friends just called him Kanu. He was a musician – a producer and composer of electronic music as well as a DJ. He was Nigerian but raised in London so he had that gorgeous English accent that took you by surprise. I loved men who took me by surprise. This was the man I would later marry – a proper wedding – the man I would one day have a daughter with.

About three months after we began seeing each other, we took our first weekend trip together to Joshua Tree. We stayed at The Roughley Manor, a quaint little English country Bed and Breakfast, about 2 miles from the Joshua Tree state park. We arrived after nightfall into the cold February desert air. After going out to dinner, I bathed in the clawfoot tub, and we lay out under the stars, keeping ourselves warm with a comforter and our body heat. My life as a battered wife, as a no esteem lost little girl, seemed about as far away as the farthest star. I had not forgotten but I had no connection to that illusion of a girl. We went back inside and made love in front of the fireplace, and then collapsed into the large four-poster bed. The stone cottage we were staying in was split into two halves and another couple slept in the other part.

It was about one am when we both fell asleep. Kanu was out cold since he had been up all night working the night before. Within the first hour of falling asleep, I woke up.

I am awakened with a start by this very high pitched sound. I sit bolt upright in bed and am startled by the intensity of this sound. I'm still very groggy but am definitely not asleep anymore. Then I get this message —I don't hear it with my ears like I did the bell, but I get the message in my head.

You are in good hands.

I feel this surge of electricity bolting throughout my entire body - it felt just like the first visit from Truth years ago in my attic bedroom in New Orleans. It was the same thing, this intense sensation of electricity moving throughout my entire body. I looked over at Kanu, who is fast asleep and I'm thinking, how can you be sleeping? Didn't you hear that sound? How can you sleep through this? But I didn't say anything and went back to sleep.

"Truth was here last night," I tell Kanu as soon as he wakes up. I had told him about other visits, and he was open and receptive to the idea. Raised by parents from Africa, the existence of spirits and a spiritual life was always present in their home. The idea that there is a spiritual world that exists right alongside our world – that idea was natural for him, so I felt safe telling him. While I was getting a little more used to these mystical experiences, I didn't for one second take for granted the blessing that had just been bestowed on me. It sent shivers down my spine and created a smile permanently fixed on my lips.

After getting dressed, we walked down to the main house for breakfast. We saw the couple who were staying in the other side, a 40-something white couple from Arizona, already sitting at the dining table eating. The innkeeper, Joanne, had made a homemade breakfast for us. While eating our quiche, Joanne told us about the long history of the house. The husband of the other couple, asked:

"Excuse me, but do you know if this place is haunted?"

Joanne smiled. "Well, people have told us stories, but I've never experienced anything myself."

The husband continued, "I don't really believe in this stuff, but last night about 2 am I had this dream and in it I was ringing this dinner bell and then all these ghosts started appearing. It was vivid and intense and like nothing I've ever dreamed before."

Both Kanu and I look at each other with big eyes. I opened my mouth and was about to speak, but then I stopped myself. The guy seemed pretty freaked out as it was. So I kept my story to myself … where would I even begin?

Epilogue

The visit, at the inn in Joshua Tree, was the last time I ever heard from Truth. I spent many years contemplating what he meant when he said, "You are in good hands". I put in way more hours than I'm willing to admit, dissecting the meaning of those five words. I initially assumed he meant the hands of my future husband, as it was the first weekend we had spent together. Why else would he deliver that message at that time? I imagined there should be some logic to spirit communication. Much later, I came to my own conclusion - he wasn't referring to Kanu's hands or even my own. I think he was referring to the hands of the universal life force, what others would call God. Life might be a mystery that I can't solve or control, but I can rest inside it. My mind doesn't need to worry about figuring it all out. I can just dance, create, love, laugh, scream, cry and trust no matter what happens, I'm in good hands.

Acknowledgments

There are many people I want to acknowledge for their support both in the experiencing and telling of this story. First, my parents - you have allowed me, without judgment, to go to the people and places that I needed to learn my lessons, and all along offered me your rock solid support. I thank you. To Jenny, I am blessed to have your generous friendship. To Phil, I am grateful for your many years of listening and for helping me to maneuver some of my trickiest moments. To George Anderson, I thank you for sharing your gift with me. To Ike, I am grateful for all your love and support over the years and for understanding that I needed to tell my story and encouraging me to write, even when the content was hard for you to hear.

I am immensely grateful to Eric, my mentor and dear friend, you helped me find my voice as an artist; this book would not exist without your gentle influence in my life. To Sam Dunn and my fellow memoir writers in her 2006 UCLA memoir workshop for first guiding me down the path of putting words to my experience. To Stephanie Birdman, I am in gratitude for your loving support and fine editor's eye. To Carol Southern and Michael Thompson, I thank you for giving me the confidence that I could publish this story. To Ron, Mary and all my soul-centered friends from USM class of 2012 for supporting and guiding me into a new, deeper level of self-love. To Liz Benedict, thank you for helping with the final editing of this story. Your wisdom, suggestions, feedback and excitement about my story helped me complete this project. I want to thank my dance tribe in LA –in the depths of my dance, I found my endless supply of courage to be and share myself. To Truth - I am eternally grateful for the gifts our relationship gave me; thank you for your visits; they changed everything for me.

Finally, to my dear Zora, you are way too young to understand this story. I hope I can instill in you a sense of how gentle, grand, and loving this world is - no matter what happens in your life.

CPSIA information can be obtained at www.ICGtesting.com
Printed in the USA
LVOW06s1703020215

425363LV00003B/255/P